Education Beyond the Coalition

Reclaiming the Agenda

Education Beyond the Coalition

Reclaiming the Agenda

Edited by Martin Allen and Patrick Ainley

ISBN   978-0-9575538-2-8

All websites quoted within this work are correct at the time   of publication. Liability cannot be accepted for any web page that expires after this point

www.radicaledbks.com

Contents

Also available from Radicaled

The Great Reversal. Young People, Education and Employment in a Declining Economy.

Martin Allen and Patrick Ainley

Education in Europe: the politics of austerity

Edited by Ken Jones

Introduction

As Christine Blower, General Secretary of the National Union of Teachers, says, 'This book is an important contribution to the debate all teachers want and need to have about what education is for'. And not only primary and secondary school teachers but their colleagues in colleges and universities who seek to articulate alternatives in the run-up to the protracted pre-election period. Many teachers at all these levels share with many parents and students widespread concerns about the current direction in which education is moving.

Already, in little more than three years, from primary to higher education, the Coalition's policies have set in train far-ranging reforms, part of what can be characterized as a *'Great Reversal'* of state education. The Education Secretary, Michael Gove, has pursued a particularly aggressive offensive. While lambasting Labour for presiding over a decade of 'falling standards', he has expanded the previous government's academies programme so far that local accountability of schools has been almost completely undermined. Gove's curriculum proposals also seek to undo years of progressive practice, reverting to the New Right philosophy of the 1980s with examination changes designed to halt two decades of rising pass rates – despite a forced U-turn on the Ebacc.

Meanwhile, the Higher Education Minister, David Willetts' policies have further turned students into 'consumers', effectively privatising universities and aiming to 'price out' many of the new generation of applicants. Yet, with sustained youth unemployment and with more and more of the few new jobs available for young people demanding degrees to get in if not to actually carry out, many school leavers have continued to sign on at uni' for debts they may never repay, despite the new panacea of 'apprenticeships' that government has offered.

Even though opinion polls show relatively low levels of popular endorsement for the Coalition's education policies, Labour has remained largely muted. To a large extent, this is because, key features of Coalition policy are extensions of Labour's previous intentions. Even when a clear change of direction has been instigated, the Party's leaders have offered little by way of a challenge. By contrast, though not having a blue-print or the magic bullet solutions that have been repeatedly foisted upon us, but also recognising that we cannot simply return to a supposed 'golden age', each chapter of this book nevertheless suggests ways forward.

The book's publication coincides with strike action called by the two main classroom teacher unions in opposition to Gove's attacks on their members' pay, conditions and pensions. This, at least potentially, represents the most serious opposition to Coalition education policies so far. As in the 1980s, the Tories know that 'defeating the teachers' is essential if their policies are to be successful. We hope that the teachers' action will both provide the space but also create the urgency for some clear educational alternatives. In fact, this would seem to be essential if the teacher unions are going to be able to rely upon support from parents. For, as Clare Kelly notes in her chapter, 'Michael Gove has positioned himself as a champion of the working class, constantly blaming inadequate teachers and bad schools for underachievement'.

Like Clare, all the contributors to this book have considerable knowledge and expertise within their particular fields. They are also campaigners committed to working outside the university seminar room to develop popular and practical alternatives. The book does not present a coherent project however. All the chapters should be considered as 'stand-alone' contributions. As a result, while there may be some overlapping, each offers a unique emphasis.

In **chapter 1**, John Yandell argues that Gove's obsessions with restoring 'rigour' in the curriculum and to assessment, are integral to his restorationist programme – a return to 'how things used to be done'. As John argues, 'rigour' is also being used to ration schooling in response to declining labour market opportunities for young people. This theme features in other contributions, which also recognise a new approach to pedagogy is needed if education is to be transformed in the interests of students.

In **chapter 2**, Clare Kelly heartened by the Cambridge Primary Review and the recent Charter for Primary Education, outlines an alternative vision for primary education which – rather than being just 'secondary preparation' penetrating primary education, emphasises personal development and participation in society. In **chapter 3** and focusing on English, Valerie Coultas provides comprehensive alternatives to Gove's elitism and prescription.

The three chapters that follow are particularly pertinent in that they address the changing relationship between young people, qualifications and the labour market, where, unlike in previous times, it can no longer be assumed that passing examinations will enable smooth transitions to secure employment because reforms to

3

education must now be linked to alternative policies for job creation and for the economy in general.

As well as providing a critique of Gove's exam changes and exposing the rationale behind them, Martin Allen in **chapter 4** argues for a general diploma for all school leavers at 18, which can be accessed at different levels but provides a mandatory core while still enabling specialisation. In **chapter 5,** Robin Simmons revisits the 1980 Macfalane proposals for 16-19 year olds and outlines an alternative way forward for FE – invariably the forgotten sector in education but arguably key to its future development. In **chapter 6** Patrick Ainley confronts the crisis in the university sector, arguing that, despite the Willetts' offensive, HE is still an important constituency for generating alternatives.

As the Coalition dismantles Local Education Authorities but with Labour still refusing to confront the implications of the private sponsorship of schools, Richard Hatcher **in chapter 7** sets out clear alternatives for restoring local accountability, increasing public participation to create an all-inclusive local school system by developing proactive LEAs. Finally in **chapter 8** and returning to the changing context in which education operates, Ken Jones provides a broader perspective on the development of alternative strategies.

Martin Allen and **Patrick Ainley,** September 2013.

Chapter 1

Curriculum, Pedagogy and Assessment: Of Rigour and Unfinished Revolutions

John Yandell

Victorian values: Gove the counter-revolutionary

Writing in the *Guardian* earlier this year, after yet another policy announcement from Michael Gove (this one was about fundamental changes to A-levels), Peter Wilby produced an elegant summary of the Education Secretary's record in office (Wilby 2013). The key to understanding Gove, suggested Wilby, lay in his past – not in some terrible childhood trauma but in his time as a journalist. Thus, whether he was proposing the purchase of a new royal yacht, dispatching copies of the Authorised Version of the Bible into all schools (with a foreword penned in his own fair hand) or insisting on a return to old-fashioned, linear A-levels, what motivated him was a keen sense of news values. In this interpretation, it was futile to look for coherence in policy, since each intervention was designed around the headlines that it would elicit: Gove was a politician on the make, and education merely a stepping-stone on the way to the top job.

Wilby's take on Gove is both psychologically plausible and tactically useful. It provides an explanation for the sheer willfulness of Gove's approach, his remarkable capacity to conjure up policies that are the wrong answers to questions that no-one is asking, his insouciant disregard for facts. Gove emerges as an ambitious, self-obsessed carpetbagger, here today and gone tomorrow. In direct contrast to his shallow, transient interest in education as soundbite lies the professional commitment of teachers, a commitment that is manifestly neither self-interested nor short-lived. That, of course, is the political value of Wilby's representation of Gove.

And yet it won't quite do, not because it's wrong about Gove's ambition or about the scattershot nature of his policies, but because it gravely understates the ideological seriousness of what is being accomplished by Gove and the Conservative-led government. As Ken Jones (2013) has argued, Gove is a counter-revolutionary, intent on completing the project that Thatcher's government started. One dimension of this project is the privatisation of education, manifested both in 'soft' forms (the creation of quasi-markets in the competition among schools; the further erosion of the role of local authorities; the expansion of the academies programme and the creation of free schools) and in the 'hard' form of handing over schools, chains of schools, the production of curricular materials and other parts of the education service on a for-profit basis to private companies. That Gove is ideologically committed to this is beyond question; his frequent lunches with Rupert Murdoch (Leigh 2012) are not, it's safe to say, evidence that they like the same kind of food but that they have a common interest in education as an immensely profitable commodity. Thus far, at least, Gove has made much more rapid progress with the soft forms; the breadth and depth of popular resistance to the longer-term aim of outright privatisation means that it is not yet realisable. After the next election, though, who knows?

In what follows, however, I want to focus not on Gove the neoliberal so much as on Gove the cultural conservative and on the dimensions of his project that relate to the curriculum, pedagogy and assessment. My interest in Gove is not some sick fascination with a particularly dangerous (and very plausible) right-wing ideologue; there is an urgent need to make an appraisal of the Conservatives' intervention in these areas and to begin to map out an adequate response.

Michael Gove has a very clear, well worked-out notion of what education is and what it is for. It is a subject to which he returns in speech after speech. Addressing an audience in Cambridge, he announced:

> 'It was an automatic assumption of my predecessors in Cabinet office that the education they had enjoyed, the culture they had benefitted from, the literature they had read, the history they had grown up learning, were all worth knowing. They thought that the case was almost so self-evident it scarcely needed to be made. To know who Pericles was, why he was important, why acquaintance with his actions, thoughts and words mattered, didn't need to be explained or justified. It was the mark of an educated person.' (Gove 2011)

To be educated, then, is to possess knowledge – particular forms of knowledge. Such knowledge is unchanging, and the business of schooling is to ensure that these stable bodies of knowledge are transmitted from one generation to the next. In the same speech, Gove makes clear that there is an established – indeed, unquestionable – hierarchy of cultural value:

> 'I am unapologetic in arguing that all children have a right to the best. And there is such as thing as the best. Richard Wagner is an artist of sublime genius and his work is incomparably more rewarding – intellectually, sensually and emotionally – than, say, the Arctic Monkeys.'

What does "knowing literature" mean?

He argues for a return to 'Victorian earnestness' and, misquoting Matthew Arnold, presents schooling as an encounter with 'the best that has been thought and written'. This Arnoldian reference reappears in the preamble to the new, Govean, national curriculum (DfE 2013, 5). And, of course, this deeply conservative view of culture and indeed of knowledge itself has direct implications for the curriculum that bears Gove's imprint. It is designed to fulfil the 'civilising mission' of schooling:

> 'In an age before structuralism, relativism and post-modernism it seemed a natural and uncomplicated thing, the mark of civilization, to want to spread knowledge, especially the knowledge of great human achievement, to every open mind. But, over time, that natural and uncomplicated belief has been undermined, over-complicated and all too often twisted out of shape.'

This wallowing in nostalgia for the simple values of a bygone age is pretty remarkable in itself. To argue that what was good enough for Gladstone is good enough for the youth of today – that knowledge of Pericles should occupy the same space in the curriculum now as then – fails to take account of the fact that the world has moved on since 1879. Should a modern curriculum limit itself to Newtonian physics, say? Is Darwinian biology possibly a little too contemporary to be contemplated? There are certainly strong correlations between Gove's version of History – *Our Island Story* – and the history that was deemed suitable for the elementary schools in the 1870s. In English, too, what we are confronted with in the new curriculum proposals is a diet of Shakespeare, Romantic poetry and Victorian novels, while texts in other media have all but disappeared.

The content of this new national curriculum is significantly more reactionary than that of any of the previous four versions. This matters, in and of itself. Within the field of English, say, there should be space for students to explore contemporary culture across different media – to read the *Simpsons* as well as Shakespeare – and to gain experience in producing new texts themselves. Questions of representation – of who and what is included, whose histories and experiences are excluded – remain vital in considering any curriculum, since any curriculum is, inevitably, a selection – and a selection motivated by particular interests.

But it would be a mistake to construe the main thrust of Gove's curricular intervention as being focused on content in and of itself – Florence Nightingale or Mary Seacole, Thomas Hardy or Choman Hardi, Dryden or Daljit Nagra. What is primarily at stake here is a question of authority. That is the force of Gove's nostalgia for Arnoldian values: he wants an education system where the value of particular artefacts, the importance of particular gobbets of knowledge is, literally, beyond question. In Gove's view of culture, value and authority are inextricably connected; thus it is that his curriculum is one of Great Books, Great Deeds, Great Scientists – and perhaps even, in a gracious nod to modernity, Great Coders. And that is why he needs to retreat to the pious certitudes of the nineteenth century – before such views of knowledge were destabilised by Einsteinian relativity, long in advance of the arrival of those pesky postmodernists.

Relativism is a real problem for Gove precisely because it presents a challenge to canonical authority. It means acknowledging different perspectives, different voices, different ways of telling the story of this island (and of other lands). It means different texts and different ways of reading the same texts. And it means asking hard questions like 'Whose knowledge is this?' and even 'Whose knowledge counts?'

In pursuit of rigour

The word that figures most prominently throughout Gove's speeches is 'rigour.' He tells his audience in Cambridge that 'mathematics, English, the sciences, foreign languages, history and geography are rigorous intellectual disciplines tested over time' – not to be confused with soft subjects and 'soft qualifications' (Gove 2011). And he tells them that he is going to make GCSEs and A levels more 'rigorous', so that they will stand comparison with exams in the 'most rigorous jurisdictions'. He tells the House of Commons that 'changes made to GCSEs under the last Government – specifically the introduction of modules and the expansion of coursework in schools – further undermined the credibility of exams – leaving young people without the rigorous education they deserved' (Gove 2012a). To address this problem, he announces, again, his determination to 'restore rigour to our examinations', to ensure 'more rigorous content' on vocational courses; in quite a short speech, the word is repeated seven times. To an audience in Brighton last year, he promises a 'more rigorous foundation stage curriculum with more emphasis on literacy and numeracy', repeats his pledge to make vocational qualifications 'rigorous and well-respected' and announces that 'we've invited top academics and university lecturers to get involved in raising standards and making examinations more rigorous' (Gove 2012b). In February 2013, talking to the Social Market Foundation, he proclaims that parents, 'especially poorer parents – want their children to get up and get on. And that means acquiring a proper rounded rigorous education':

> 'Visit the most exclusive pre-prep and prep schools in
> London – like Wetherby in Notting Hill – where artistic and

creative leaders like Stella McCartney send their children –
and you will find children learning to read using traditional
phonic methods, times tables and poetry learnt by heart,
grammar and spelling rigorously policed, the narrative of
British history properly taught. And on that foundation those
children then move to schools like Eton and Westminster –
where the medieval cloisters connect seamlessly to the
corridors of power.' (Gove 2013)

You get the picture. Rigour matters. And it's a good thing. A very
good thing. But what does it mean?

Its ever-presence might make it tempting to conclude that 'rigour'
doesn't mean anything at all, that it is the perfect floating signifier,
untethered to any point of reference in the real world. But that
would be to underestimate its value to Gove. It's worth looking at
the ideological work that 'rigour' does for him. First, it has
immense nostalgic power – and Gove is a politician who
understands the power of nostalgia. Rigour is strongly associated
with tradition, with how things used to be done. Thus, it is a quality
that needs to be 'restored' to assessment processes, to curricula, to
teaching methods: in the past, exams were rigorous and reliable,
subjects weren't 'soft' (like media studies) but rigorous (like
maths), and teaching used traditional methods, which were,
obviously, more rigorous than the progressive ones that have crept
in since 1967 (Plowden and all that). And that is the second facet of
Govean rigour: it is a stick with which to beat the bugbear of
progressivism. There is nothing new about this – it has been open
season on progressive practice since Callaghan's speech at Ruskin
in 1976. Gove's attack on 'The Progressive Betrayal' (Gove 2013)
aligns him just as much with Blair as it does with Thatcher or
Major. Even so, Gove's attachment to rigour gives him the edge on

the soft anti-progressives who preceded him. Like his insistence that grammar and spelling should be 'rigorously policed', it suggests something of the depth of his attachment to authority – the authority of the subject disciplines, the authority of the exam board, the authority of the school as an institution – and (sometimes) the authority of the teacher (but not, as has already become clear, when it comes to matters of assessment).

Rationing education

There is, moreover, a third aspect to Gove's advocacy of rigour that marks a breach with New Labour and a further intensification of the Thatcherite counter-revolution: rigour is a euphemism for rationing. Gove's belief in the virtue of rationing isn't immediately obvious from what he says. It is, on the other hand, an absolutely central feature of his government's policy, demonstrated in every phase of education from the scrapping of EMA (education maintenance allowance) and the rise in university tuition fees to the closure of Sure Start centres. The effect of all of these measures is to make it harder for working-class children and students to gain access to or to thrive within the arena of formal educational provision: it is to ration education. But that's not all. Committed to rigorous assessment, Gove wages war on 'grade inflation'. What this means is placing an arbitrary cap on what students can achieve. It means the return of norm-referencing in place of criterion-referencing. And the effects of this were seen last summer, when tens of thousands of GCSE students ended up with lower grades than they had been predicted because the exam boards, under pressure from Ofqual, raised the crucial C/D threshold. For the students affected, this had material consequences: it meant that many of them could not progress on to the A-level courses that they had chosen.

What happened in the summer of 2012 was a stark case of grade deflation. The grade boundaries were manipulated to satisfy a higher power's arbitrary judgments about how many students should be awarded a particular grade. As Ofqual's own report revealed (Ofqual 2012, 10), it was decided that the proportion of students who were awarded grade C or above should be adjusted downwards because, among other reasons, there were more private school students entered for alternative qualifications (the iGCSE, say), and so they made the assumption that the calibre of the cohort entered for the GCSE would be poorer than in the previous year. And, as the *TES* revealed (28 September 2012), the students who were worst affected by the shift in the grade boundaries were working-class and minority ethnic students.

This wasn't an accident or technical difficulty; it was a moment when the trajectory of government policy in education was starkly revealed. It was the direct consequence of Gove's commitment to rigour, because what rigour means, in the context of high-stakes assessment, is ensuring that there are failures. There is nothing new about the education system functioning as a sorting mechanism, a means whereby structural inequalities in society are reproduced. There is something new, however, in having a government that is so intensely relaxed about this. In education, as in so many other areas of government intervention, austerity provides the cloak for policies that are ideologically motivated: for Gove, rationing is not an unfortunate by-product of rigour but part of its *raison d'être*.

This rationing policy, as Martin Allen suggests in a later chapter, aligns education with pan-European economic reality. At a time of mass youth unemployment, the New Labour pieties of a 'knowledge economy' have a distinctly hollow ring: in the current climate, schooling simply cannot be sold to students on the basis of a promise that compliance will lead to credentialisation (good grades) and credentialisation will lead to economic advancement (good – graduate? – jobs). So Gove has produced the education policy for austerity Britain. He may talk about the importance of children knowing about place value, but what he really means is the importance of knowing their place. To this end, it makes perfect sense to present the curricular subjects as authoritative, as the repository of stable, established, canonical knowledge and to present teaching as the transmission of this authoritative, authorised knowledge, 'the best that has been thought and said'.

As Martin Allen also argues, an adequate alternative to the current government's policies would entail a radically different economic policy. Within the narrower sphere of education, though, there are vitally important arguments to be won. Let's start with assessment. Gove's preference is for the terminal examination, with candidates being required to write long essays (Ofqual 2013b). (As I understand it, the quill pen remains optional at this stage!) This, like his version of a Hirschian 'core knowledge' curriculum, tests a very specific set of skills and is preparation for almost nothing in the world beyond the exam hall. (For one job, however, it offers the perfect apprenticeship – and that is Gove's old job as a leader writer for the *Times*. It does, however, seem a little perverse to construct an entire national assessment regime on so narrowly vocational a base.) Modular tests, retakes and coursework have all been anathematised (so has the tiering of exam papers – but that's a different story; tiers were forced on us in GCSE by the Major government in the early 1990s).

There seem to be three central assumptions underpinning this retreat to the 1950s. First, teachers are not to be trusted. This appears very plainly in Ofqual's recent pronouncement against the inclusion of the assessment of speaking and listening in the GCSE English so as 'to make the qualifications more robust, and more resistant to pressure from school accountability systems' (Ofqual 2013a, 2). Or, in plain language, teachers might be tempted to give their students a higher mark because they – the teachers – and their schools tend to be judged on the basis of GCSE results. Second, there is the belief that retaking an exam is not quite cricket – sort of cheating, really. Quite why this should be so in relation to A-levels or GCSEs, but not driving tests, isn't immediately apparent. Underpinning this belief, I suspect, is a particularly nasty sort of innatism – a view of intelligence as fixed, a given, which the examination process simply reveals. This involves a profoundly anti-educational view of the student – a deeply pessimistic rejection of the possibility of improvement, of learning. Third, all Gove's talk of rigour betrays a staggeringly naive faith in the reliability of any assessment system. It treats some forms of assessment as offering a transparent window on the individual subject. That isn't, of course, what assessment is or how it works. Assessment is always imprecise, always a social process.

Let's go back a moment to the controversy about the GCSE English results in 2012. Part of the reason for the widespread anger among teachers was the gap between students' predicted and actual grades. In most spheres of life, when we talk about predictions, we measure these against actual events. So the weather forecast is a prediction about what the weather will be like, at a particular time and in a particular place. The forecast uses evidence, of various kinds and varying degrees of sophistication. The question of the accuracy of a weather forecast is easily determined: we can test it out by what actually happens. Did it rain today? Likewise predictions about horse-racing are testable against the race itself. If I give you a tip for the 4.30 at Newbury, you are entitled to judge the usefulness and the accuracy of the tip, and probably of me as a tipster, by what actually happens in the 4.30 at Newbury.

Now, the commonsense approach to predicted GCSE grades would be the same as outlined above. An English teacher predicts a grade C for her student; he gets a grade D; the prediction was wrong, demonstrably, because the prediction did not match what actually happened in the exam. But this is nonsense. A GCSE exam is not like the 4.30 at Newbury. The claims that a GCSE result purports to make about a student are not limited to what happened in an exam hall on a particular afternoon in June; they are claims about what that student knows and can do, in relation to a range of texts and practices that have been gathered together under the heading of 'English'. In fact – in the real world where people talk, read and write a variety of different texts for different audiences and purposes – that GCSE student's English teacher is in the best position to say what that student knows and can do. In this situation, then, the prediction shouldn't really be construed as a prediction at all; it is a statement based on detailed, in-depth professional knowledge, from someone who has been able to build up a picture of that student's learning and development over time. The teacher has a mass of evidence on which to base this professional judgement – evidence much more robust because it is more plentiful and also because it is much more diverse than the evidence that can be provided by a single exam. If this is true for secondary students, it is even more obvious in primary schools, where six-year-olds are now forced to experience the farce that is the phonics test – a test that bears precious little relation to any literacy practice and that provides no useful information on learning.

I am all in favour of robust accountability systems, as Ofqual might put it. But what we need – and need to argue for – are forms of assessment that do justice to the breadth, complexity and sheer messiness of learning, forms of assessment that are not so easily reducible to accountancy, forms of assessment that involve giving an account of learning over time. Teachers are in a position to be able to provide precisely this kind of rich, rigorous accountability. The problem with Gove's claim to be implementing more rigorous assessment is that it's simply not true. What he's doing is imposing cruder, less reliable tests – tests that will, however, be well suited to the task of sorting students and rationing success.

It might seem that arguing for the centrality of teacher assessment is hopelessly Utopian. But in many other countries – including such 'high-performing jurisdictions' as Finland – it's a reality. The outlier, even now, is England. And, with the raising of the education participation age, there is absolutely no good reason for maintaining any form of external, centralised assessment system at 16. Other countries manage fine without one.

Curriculum, pedagogy and the problem of knowledge

In the final part of this chapter, I want to return to the question of the curriculum. Gove's claims to rigour here should properly be subjected to ridicule. There's nothing rigorous about a curriculum that resolutely turns its back on the realities – sophisticated, layered, intertextual realities – of twenty-first century digital textual practices and retreats into the imagined safety of a literary canon. There's nothing rigorous about a curriculum that is constructed of factoids, neatly arranged in lists. There's nothing rigorous about a curriculum that pretends to an ignorance of theory, of debate, of the contestation of ideas. What is produced is a particularly disreputable instance of the alchemy described by

Thomas Popkewitz:

> 'The curriculum of schools performs an alchemy on...
> disciplinary knowledge. The specific relations from which
> historians or physicists, for example, produce knowledge
> undergoes a magical change. Whereas disciplines involve
> competing sets of ideas about research... school subjects tend
> to treat knowledge as uncontested and unabiguous content for
> children to learn or solve problems with.' (Popkewitz 1998,
> 27)

This content-driven curriculum is, however, very fashionable.
Shaped in the image of Hirsch's (1996) 'core knowledge', it can
also draw succour from recent interventions by Frank Furedi
(2009) and Michael Young (2008, 2009). Furedi conceptualises
education as the 'intergenerational transmission of knowledge'
(2009, 48). He attacks progressive education from Dewey onwards
for its neglect of this duty, teachers for being complicit in the
erosion of adult authority and New Labour for policies such as
Every Child Matters, which he sees as an unwarrantable intrusion
of social engineering into the business of schooling. Young,
meanwhile, though ready to concede that there might be a place for
more progressive, child-centred pedagogy, insists that schools
should be responsible for the transmission of 'powerful knowledge'
– knowledge that is 'objective in ways that transcend the historical
conditions of its production' (2008, 28). Young's argument needs
to be taken seriously. And yet, for all his attempts to distinguish his
position from that of the neocons like Gove, he has a similar
attachment to transcendent value: if for Gove it is self-evident that
Wagner is 'greater' than the Arctic Monkeys, for Young it is
equally clear that Jane Austen is worth studying (because her
novels are 'timeless in the moral and relationship issues that they
explore' [2008, 23]), whereas *Holby City* is not.

18

There are, it seems to me, two fundamental problems with this conception of knowledge, and hence of the school curriculum. The first is, in a sense, a matter of emphasis. If, under the weight of relentless policy intervention, all attention is directed to the content of the curriculum, what becomes marginalised is pedagogy – by which I mean both questions of how children learn and, inextricably connected with this, the social relations of the classroom. One of the great strengths of the progressive tradition in education is that it has attended to – and problematised – these questions. The conservative tradition, on the other hand, has tended to dismiss them, for the reason that they simply don't figure if one retains an unshakeable belief in the authority of knowledge and hence the authority of the teacher who transmits the knowledge. The conservative tradition thus involves a deeply reductive view of the nature of teachers' expertise. Teachers' professional knowledge does not reside simply in content knowledge – knowledge of gerunds or gravity – but in deeply situated knowledge of how children learn – and of particular learners (Heilbronn and Yandell 2010). So, to take one example, teachers – particularly primary teachers – understand the immensely powerful contribution that play can make to learning and development.

The second problem is to do with the conception of knowledge itself, in that it abstracts knowledge from culture and history, as if knowledge were a thing, a commodity to be acquired, rather than a process that involves historical agents – people with particular interests, in particular and always evolving social relations, people making meaning out of the resources that are available to them. This different conception of knowledge may seem far removed from the day-to-day realities of the classroom, but it is crucial to the development of an adequate alternative model of curriculum and pedagogy. It matters because it constitutes an entirely different orientation towards the learners. Whereas the content-driven curriculum constructs students as deficits (they are the empty vessels to be filled with the powerful knowledge that schooling offers), this dialectical conception of knowledge insists on the agency and the interests of the learners – not just as a starting-point (establishing prior knowledge, say) but as centrally implicated in all educational processes and activities. In this version of schooling, curriculum ceases to be something to be delivered from on high; it becomes a process, enacted (and contested) among a group of interested participants.

This moment presents us with a real opportunity to engage in a serious debate about what education is for. In the period of New Labour, however specious the rhetoric of the knowledge economy and the standards agenda was, it achieved a kind of hegemony. Teachers' sense of professional identity became enmeshed in the dominant accountability measures of high-stakes testing and Ofsted criteria. While each successive cohort attained better grades, while teachers' ever more fine-tuned efforts to meet the targets and maximise potential seemed to bear fruit, there was plausibility to the myth of school improvement. Now, though, as teachers are confronted with rigour and rationing and a headlong retreat to the Victorian era, as it becomes obvious that students' learning and development simply cannot be mapped onto imposed curricula and are not reflected in the academic credentials they are awarded, there might be a space to argue for something different – an approach to teaching and learning that takes seriously the interests of the learners. All of them.

When asked what he thought of European civilisation, Gandhi replied that he thought it would be a very good idea (or so the story goes). Something of the same might be said of comprehensive education. It won't do to regard it as a failed social democratic experiment, unfit for the rigours of twenty-first-century life. Rather, we should recognise that it is a vital part of our own unfinished revolution, a transformation of education that cannot be accomplished through changes to institutional structures alone, a transformation that requires the fundamental rethinking of the content and pedagogic processes of schooling.

References

Department for Education (2013) *The national curriculum in England:*
Framework document, July 2013, available online at
https://www.gov.uk/government/uploads/system/uploads/attachm
ent_data/file/210969/NC_framework_document_-_FINAL.pdf,
accessed 6 August 2013.

Furedi, F. (2009) *Wasted: why education isn't educating*. New York & London: Continuum.

Gove, M. (2011) speech at Cambridge University, 24 November 2011, available online at
http://www.education.gov.uk/inthenews/speeches/a00200373/mic
hael-gove-to-cambridge-university, accessed 13 September 2012.

Gove, M. (2012a) Examination Reform Speech, 17 September 2012, House of Commons, available online at
http://www.conservatives.com/News/Speeches/2012/09/Michael_
Gove_Exam_Reform_Speech.aspx, accessed 12 August 2013.

Gove, M. (2012b) speech at Brighton College, 10 May 2012,

available online at
http://www.politicshome.com/uk/article/53168/michael_goves_sp
eech_to_brighton_college.html, accessed 13 September 2012.

Gove, M. (2013) 'The Progressive Betrayal', speech to the
Social Market Foundation, 5 February 2013, available online
at http://www.smf.co.uk/media/news/michael-gove-speaks-
smf/, accessed 12 August 2013.

Heilbronn, R. & Yandell, J. (eds 2010) *Critical Practice in
Teacher Education: a study of professional learning*. London:
Institute of Education.

Hirsch, E.D. (1996) *The Schools We Need and Why We Don't
Have Them*, New York: Doubleday.

Jones, K. (2013) 'The English Educational Conjuncture',
paper for the Goldsmiths Seminar on Educational Conflict in
Western Europe, 17 May 2013, Goldsmiths, University of
London.

Leigh, D. (2012) 'The schools crusade that links Michael Gove
to Rupert Murdoch', *The Guardian*, 27 February 2012,
available online at
http://www.theguardian.com/politics/2012/feb/26/schools-
crusade-gove-murdoch, accessed 12 August 2013.

Ofqual (2012) *GCSE English Awards 2012: A Regulatory
Report*, available online at www.ofqual.gov.uk/files/2012-08-
31-gcse-english-awards-2012-a-regulatory-report.pdf,
accessed 30 September 2012.

Ofqual (2013a) *Consultation on the Removal of Speaking and Listening Assessment from GCSE English and GCSE English Language* [Ofqual 13/5274]. Available online at http://www.ofqual.gov.uk/files/2013-04-25-gcse-english-consultation-on-the-removal-of-speaking-and-listening.pdf, accessed 19 July 2013.

Ofqual (2013b) *GCSE Reform Consultation* [Ofqual 13/5292], available online at http://comment.ofqual.gov.uk/gcse-reform-june-2013/, accessed 19 July 2013.

Popkewitz, T. S. (1998) *Struggling for the Soul: the politics of schooling and the construction of the teacher*. New York & London: Teachers College Press.

Wilby, P. (2013) 'A-level reforms: Michael Gove's bid to grab headlines will merely narrow pupils' learning', *The Guardian*, 28 January 2013, available online at http://www.theguardian.com/commentisfree/2013/jan/27/michael-gove-headline-tory-leader-education, accessed 12 August 2013.

Young, M. (2008) *Bringing Knowledge Back In: from social constructivism to social realism in the sociology of education*, London and New York: Routledge.

Young, M. (2009) 'What are schools for?' In *Knowledge, Values and Educational Policy*, ed. H. Daniels, H. Lauder & J. Porter. London: Routledge, 11-18.

Chapter 2

Primary Education: From Market Forces to Personal Development

Clare Kelly

At the heart of the educational process lies the child (DES 1967).

The national curriculum provides pupils with an introduction to the essential knowledge that they need to be educated citizens. It introduces pupils to the best that has been thought and said; and helps engender an appreciation of human creativity and achievement (DfE 2013).

Introduction

These statements represent opposing paradigms of primary education. The first from the influential Plowden Report, published in 1967 and the second from the introduction to the recently redrafted proposals for the National Curriculum for England. They represent divergent views on the role of the child in their learning and the most recent poses questions about the purposes and outcomes of education. Locating statements that refer to children in Coalition documents and Gove's speeches proves to be problematic. The emphasis is on teachers, subjects, schools, leadership, behaviour, initial teacher education, standards and accountability, but not the child, who seems to have got curiously lost in the discourse on 'excellence'.

The government's proposals for assessment and accountability (DfE 2013, 2) can help to clarify the Coalition's position by confirming 'the single most important outcome that any primary school should strive to achieve is making sure as many of its pupils as possible are "secondary ready" by the time they leave', which fits comfortably with Cameron and Clegg's declaration in the foreword to the Schools White Paper *The Importance of Teaching* (2010, 3) 'in the education debate what really matters is how we're doing compared with our international competitors'. The government's intention for the connection between education and the labour market is clear.

The neoliberal agenda, developed and sustained by New Labour and intensified by the Coalition government since 2010, has seen the processes of education diminished to dogma and the promotion of a view of teaching and learning that is reductionist and directly linked to the shaping of the economy. The marketing of education as a commodity has led to increased diversification of schooling based on semi-privatisation and the spectre of running schools for profit, the introduction of free schools and the expansion of the academy programme to include more primary schools, often against the wishes of parents and governors. An alternative view of primary education cannot be inserted into this regime, but demands wider reforms including a reconsideration of the relationship between education and the state.

This chapter will argue that the neoliberal agenda for education, evident in the UK and the West at the end of the twentieth century, but consolidated in the twenty-first, has damaged schooling in England in the primary and early years and an alternative construct of education as personal development is necessary. Personal development is not envisaged here as foregrounding individualism but enabling growth of the whole child intellectually, culturally, socially, politically and emotionally to become a confident, independent and critical learner capable of participating as a citizen in an inclusive and socially just society. It is argued that such a shift would require cultural, structural and curricular changes if primary and early years educators are to offer children opportunities to learn and develop in relation to principles of equality and fairness, and will depend for its actuality on the formation of alliances between parents, trade unionists and others interested in the quality and promise of state education.

The centralised curriculum and the distinctiveness of primary and early years education

Plowden, published almost 50 years ago, although criticised for its dependence on Piagetian theory, was ground-breaking with its emphasis on a flexible curriculum, the significance of the educational environment, the importance of heuristic learning and a requirement to evaluate rather than measure progress. It was followed almost a decade later by the Bullock Report with its well-reported assertion that 'no child should be expected to cast off the language and culture of the home as he (*sic*) crosses the school threshold' (DES 1975, 286). Although neither of these reports is directly applicable to the present era, many of their principles are kept alive by those who argue for a child-centred view of education, demonstrating that there are valuable lesssons to be learnt from the history of education policy, taking account of what was successful.

One less helpful legacy of Plowden has been its use as a reference for concerns and misrepresentations from traditionalists and the right-wing press about 'trendy' practices and the outcomes of progressive methods that endure to the present day. Yet studies show there is little evidence to suggest the validity of these claims and that nationally, teachers and schools did not wholeheartedly embrace the new ways of working introduced in the report (Galton *et al* 1980).

Labour Prime Minister Callaghan's Ruskin speech in 1976 marked a move from autonomy to centralisation, to facilitate, among other matters, the link between education and economic prosperity. Little more than a decade later, the Education Reform Act introduced a subject-based entitlement National Curriculum assessed by levels, and monitored by tests. These policies had significant implications for primary education with the downward pressure from a secondary school curriculum model and the requirement to test children aged 7 and 11, which necessitated a shift from child-centered practices, introduced a concern for 'coverage' and established ability grouping (Pollard *et al* 1994). Such changes impacted significantly on teachers' workload and conditions and were the subject of action by NUT members; the boycott of SATs in 1993 to 1995 won the end of league tables for seven year olds.

Early Years and Primary school teachers know the context of their school and quickly get to know the children in their class because of the concentrated period of time they spend with them each day. Establishing relationships with children and their families enables teachers to recognise the complexity of factors both outside and inside school that impact on learner identities and can affect children's progress. Teachers frequently express frustration at the regulation of practices that should be based on their professional judgements and knowledge of children as individuals. Early years practitioners are familiar with the rationale for planning for children's learning based on understanding their interests and concerns developed through close observation and partnerships with families. Yet Elizabeth Truss, Minister for Education and Childcare and a former member of the right-wing think tank, Civitas, deprecating these principles, denounced 'chaotic' pre-school settings that allow children to 'do what they want all day' when they should be 'paying attention to the teacher and learning good manners', so they can 'sit still and listen when they get to primary school' (Chapman & Chorley 2013). Her comments promote compliance and passive learning for the youngest children and demonstrate the pressure to correspond with expectations for statutory schooling. She is readily supported by Michael Wilshaw, Chief Inspector of Schools, who condemned the breadth of assessment represented in the current early years profile document, preferring instead a more rigid regime that linked to KS1, particularly in relation to numeracy and literacy (Ofsted 2013).

The ideological project embodied in educational polices since the ERA has introduced increased regulation of primary education and rapid changes that have contributed to a climate of uncertainty for schools. The threat of failure: for children, teachers, schools and education departments in universities, maintained by the government through policing by Ofsted, reductive league tables and a policy of public naming and shaming, is ever present. The current climate constrains risk-taking and experimentation and obstructs creative approaches to learning and teaching that could result in innovation and originality.

Neoliberal educational policies and inequality

Michael Gove has positioned himself as a champion of the working class, consistently blaming inadequate teachers and bad schools for underachievement rather than an unequal system. In the introduction to the *Importance of Teaching* and in subsequent speeches, he promotes social mobility through meritocratic policies that are characterised as enabling working-class children to enter Oxbridge.

Making full use of his background as a journalist for News International, Gove exploits the media to publicly misrepresent and belittle educationalists, 'unions and their allies' who oppose his policies, as having low aspirations for children, distorting their arguments as acceptance of poor standards and mediocrity, branding them as 'the enemies of promise' (Gove 2013). Predictably, the complexities of the relationships between class, social disadvantage, educational opportunity and family circumstances intersected by ethnicity, gender and disability, do not feature in Gove's vision of 'equality of opportunity'. And although he frequently speaks about underachievement of the 'poorest children', the austerity agenda with which he is complicit leads to cuts in benefits, the movement of families from their homes and away from their local schools and reduces welfare provision and state responsibility for vulnerable groups, thus exacerbating economic and social divisions. The effect is indicated by the Child Poverty Action Group's report (CPAG 2013) that 3.5 million (27%) of children are currently living in poverty and a further 600,000 are expected to be added to that number by 2015 under current government policies.

Gove does not appear to show interest in the learning of other groups either. His voice was not heard defending bilingual children and those from minority ethnic backgrounds who might require language or other forms of support, when the Coalition government cut funding to local authorities for ethnic minority achievement support services and many EMASS teams were made redundant nationally. The valued expertise and experience represented by members of these teams were lost to teachers, schools and vulnerable groups of children.

Indeed, Gove reinforces an elitist view of languages. In the National Curriculum for 2014 language learning is valorised as a liberation from insularity, providing an openness to other cultures. Yet in the same document there is no acknowledgement that 17.5% of children in state primary schools speak more than one language and are likely to possess the advantages that are promoted by the new language curriculum. Their strengths are devalued as they are included in a section in the document on special educational needs. Researchers, such as Thomas & Collier (1997), have been arguing for many years that learning English as a new language does not constitute a special educational need and adopting a deficit model is likely to affect children's cognitive and linguistic development.

Before the Coalition, New Labour implemented some education policies that were designed to address disadvantage and promote diversity. The high profile Sure Start programme provided integrated services for families and pre-school experience for children through Children's Centres. Despite mixed evaluations of its overall success, Sure Start did not yield the expected cognitive gains for children and lacked the potential to address the complexity of factors involved in disadvantage. Wider welfare reforms on tax and benefits focussed on more deep-rooted issues leading to a reduction in levels of poverty between 1998/9 and 2011/12 (CPAG 2013).

Other enlightened polices such as *Excellence and Enjoyment* (DfES 2003), set out opportunities and provided models for primary schools to work creatively and make links with parents and the local community. The following year, *Every Child Matters* promoted children's safety and well-being and was responsible for major changes to school practices. ECM was used by some schools to promote diversity, according to Sir Keith Ajegbo the author of *Diversity & Citizenship,* which set out the importance of teaching about identity and difference and reiterated the fundamental role of citizenship education.

New Labour's imperative to develop social cohesion, if loosely defined, did not underestimate the pressures for schools of building relationships of trust with local communities based on their unique historical and cultural contexts. Kathryn Riley (2013) has shown how managing the interface between education policy and community challenges was exacting and caused tensions for school leaders.

The inherent problem for primary schools was a contradiction between the freedoms implicit in these reports which endorsed the development of schools as communities to promote inclusion and value diversity and the constraints of a prescriptive curriculum for maths and literacy, a coercive high-stakes testing regime and the threat of punitive Ofsted inspections. New Labour's policies were not sufficiently expansive or connected. The contradictions apparent in them appeared to reflect the tensions and divisions within the Labour Party.

The paradox of the National Curriculum in primary schools
The National Curriculum, introduced under the Thatcher government, was upheld by New Labour on coming to power. They prioritised 'the basics' by unveiling the National Literacy Strategy for primary schools 1998 and the Numeracy Strategy a year later, which were both superseded by the Primary National Strategy (PNS) in 2006. The National Curriculum was revised in 2000 and

reviewed in 2009 to accommodate these changes, but it was these *non-statutory,* highly regulated programmes, that were policed by Ofsted and enforced by local authority personnel, which formed the basis of teachers' planning. Government initiatives appeared to overrule the National Curriculum. For example, when the requirement to teach synthetic phonics was introduced nationally, with no consensus, the English programmes of study for reading at Key Stage 1 were adjusted, without publicity, to remove references to use of a range of reading strategies, most notably, those that relied on meaning or language (Wyse & Styles 2007).

The description of the National Curriculum at Key Stage 1 and Key Stage 2 as 'broad and balanced' and 'an entitlement' is apparent in successive revisions, with the exception of the proposals for 2014 which does not include such emancipatory language. These terms, often repeated, became increasingly meaningless as primary teachers focused on numeracy and literacy, which represented in effect, the much narrower offer of number, reading and writing, spending every morning on these 'core' subjects. Teachers in years 2 and 6, adjusted their teaching to fit the narrow demands of the SATs tests (Harlen 2007). Consequently, it became a struggle to incorporate other areas of the curriculum such as art, geography, music or PE, which were officially relegated in 1999 to the status of 'foundation subjects'.

The Coalition's proposals for the National Curriculum 2014 maintain this hierarchical subject-based construct, validating teaching as the transmission of knowledge and learning as memorisation and the accumulation of skills. The programmes of study channel primary aged children's energies into the rigidity of mechanical learning and underestimate their capabilities, for example in relation to multimodal literacy practices. It ignores their concerns about sustainability and climate change and interest in politics and world and community events, evident from research (Warwick 2008). By abolishing the citizenship curriculum and enforcing the promotion of British cultural heritage through other subjects, there is a danger the 2014 curriculum will deny primary-aged children channels for discussion of issues that are important to them. At the time of writing, a Charter for Primary Education (2013) has been drawn up and circulated by a group of teachers, parents, authors, academics and others which sets out key principles for teaching and an alternative construction of young children as involved learners.

The high level of prescription in NC 2014 does not match Gove's intention set out in the 2010 White Paper to 'free our teachers from constraint and improve their professional status and authority' DFE, 8). It is unlikely that primary teachers will feel liberated to make judgments about the balance between subjects, because they know that the next Ofsted inspector who visits their class will examine their teaching of the micro-managed English and Maths programmes of study. In addition, success in recently instituted tests of nonsense words for six year olds and decontextualised tests of spelling, punctuation and grammar for eleven year olds will demand coaching and drilling. The primary curriculum cannot be divorced from a coercive accountability agenda: assessment through targets and testing, punitive monitoring by Ofsted and professional liability through published league tables.

The content of the National Curriculum has been responsible for major changes to the organisation of schools, teachers' practices and pupils' experiences, but its history also shows it is not the monolithic document it is made out to be and in the past it has been used selectively, manipulated and ignored. Perhaps the biggest contradiction for the latest version is that as the expansion of academies and free schools continues, the NC will apply to progressively fewer schools, since these establishments are not required to follow it.

An alternative model of education

Deeper questions about the purposes of primary education must be addressed to sever the link between the shaping of the work force and the day to day experiences of young children. A curriculum that reflects an understanding of education as the development of the whole child will have no place for what Robin Alexander termed the hegemony of the core subjects. It will restore a genuinely broader offer, including a central position for the arts as both valuable in their own right, in addition to providing the basis for affective and intellectual development. Official constructions of teaching and learning will be realigned with theory and classroom-based research so that learning is seen as a human social experience and not a race to reach superficial targets of quantifiable knowledge.

The Cambridge Primary Review (Alexander 2009) made comprehensive recommendations for all aspects of primary education following extensive research at regional and national level. Its recommendations were wide ranging, covering ten educational themes emphasising the importance of a rich curriculum and the autonomy of teachers to make decisions about their practice in relation to their knowledge of children and their context, advocating also that formal schooling should not begin until age six, corresponding to international practice. The Review's conclusions were discounted if not ignored by the New Labour government, which had commissioned its own review of the National Curriculum which was in the process of implementation in schools when they lost the election in 2010. Nevertheless, the Cambridge Review, albeit with some reservations (Drummond 2010) is a reference point for an alternative vision for primary education based on democratic principles.

Studies of primary education have shown the quality of interaction and communication between children and their teachers is a significant factor in improving learning experiences and supporting progress (Wyse *et al* 2008). Moving children through a curriculum overloaded with objectives restricts time for questioning, exploring ideas and developing reflective responses. There is much to be learnt from schools who have worked to create a broader experience for children through, for example, co-construction of the curriculum in the LB Wandsworth or arts-based learning in the LB Newham or the introduction of Forest Schools in many areas nationally.

In these schools and others striving to develop creative practices, the processes of learning are foregrounded. Dialogic teaching, learning through play, children's active engagement, exploration and enquiry in a collaborative environment offer children and teachers approaches to learning that should be the norm rather than the celebrated exceptions they are at present.

A dialogue about the fundamental role and practices of primary education would need to involve teachers and other educationalists, and as such has the potential to restore the status of teaching as a professional activity. Providing support for teacher-led research that takes account of children in the classroom and the community of the school is a more effective way to develop new practices that improve children's educational experience than scaling up initiatives from one context with the assumption they are applicable for universal translation (Levin 2013).

The development of literacy in early years and primary classrooms requires urgent reconsideration to prevent more children being subjected to the outcomes of an instrumental, skills-based conception of reading and writing. The Independent Review of Reading, commissioned by New Labour in 2006, was neither independent nor about reading, only phonics. Conducted by Jim Rose, a former HMI but not a literacy or early years specialist, it recommended the wholesale introduction of systematic synthetic phonics, based mainly on visits to ten schools and spurious evidence from two studies in Scotland (Wyse & Styles 2007). Learning to read was characterised as developing decoding skills and since that time a rigid programme of phonics teaching has dominated early years and key stage 1 classrooms to the exclusion of meaning-based approaches, despite many teachers' professional knowledge and experience telling them otherwise.

Reductive approaches to literacy do not take account of the complexities involved in becoming literate in the 21st century, meet the needs of children or instill a sense of the possibilities and personal satisfactions that can come from reading and writing. The most recent international comparisons of the reading achievement and attitudes of 9 -10 year olds (Twist *et al* 2011) show that results for England point to a tail of underachievement. Although most able readers were among the best in the survey, the weakest were amongst the worst. Children's attitudes to reading were less positive in England than the international average.

Henrietta Dombey (2011) draws on evidence from a series of studies in the US to show that successful reading comes from incorporating word identification skills with attention to meaning, engaging in quality interactions with adults, a high level of child engagement and close monitoring of individual progress. Restoring talk at the heart of literacy, introducing children to a range of texts and authors through personal reading and reading aloud, encouraging preferences and developing critical and reflective responses are successful practices that are grounded in research (O'Sullivan & McGonigle 2010) and have the potential to connect with children's lives outside of the classroom to make them truly literate.

Another area for urgent attention is Citizenship. Seen as irrelevant by Gove and removed from the Primary Curriculum 2014, it should occupy a central place in the curriculum and feature again in ITE and Continuing Professional Development (CPD) programmes for teachers. Education as development brings with it the responsibility to prepare children to participate as citizens in a society that promotes social justice and shared values. Enabling respect for difference and recognition of diversity as strength can start with the youngest children. Talking about children's cultures, heritages, languages and multiethnic identities is an important starting point for anti-racist education and can lead to both links with local communities and an understanding of global citizenship.

The Coalition government has continued to dismiss issues of equality that affect learning outcomes for children, except in a narrow way as previously discussed. Children bring understanding and interests to school that are rooted in the lives of their families and communities (Kelly 2010). Education for development would mean children share their cultures and languages in the classroom to demonstrate their strengths, enrich the school community and establish that making links with knowledge and experience from home is an important part of the learning experience. The challenge for the early years and primary teacher is to help children draw on these familiar experiences to make connections with school learning and its more abstract use of language and other symbolic forms.

Accountability

Accountability is part of the democratic process: teachers and schools should be accountable to the children they teach and their families, to the local community and to the public who fund education. However, the current audit culture and proliferation of targets and league tables in the guise of public accountability, serve the short-term needs of politicians. Diane Ravitch (2010) has shown how high stakes bureaucratic assessment procedures, distort teaching, impoverish children's experiences and restrict their learning. An alternative view of assessment which draws on teachers' judgements and validates the status of formative assessment, which can also be used summatively, takes account of the complexities of the learning process, which is currently essentialised and numbered. The abolition of targets and testing would prevent the labelling of children and could reverse the ubiquitous growth of ability grouping in primary schools that Susan Hart and colleagues (2004) have shown facilitates the systematic reproduction of inequalities.

The ERA established parents as consumers and that role has been intensified with the diversification of schooling and increased competition for places. At a recent meeting about education policy, the parent of a primary-aged child at an academy spoke of her frustration at receiving regular numerical summaries of her child's attainment. A conception of education as development would as many schools already recognise, promote an ethos of working with parents who want to know about the quality of their children's experience and relationships as well as their progress.

Colin Richards (2010), building on the work of the Cambridge Review, suggests a three level alternative accountability framework overseen by an independent body which would use sampling discretely to survey standards nationally across all curriculum areas. School level evaluation by suitably qualified and experienced personnel would involve staff and take account of the school's self-evaluation and improvement processes. Judgments of individual progress would take the form of a combination of on-going teacher assessment and summative measures to include children's attitudes to learning, although the argument that this would also involve testing is problematic.

Richards' system would give parents and the wider community information about children's progress and the quality of schooling while acknowledging schools' understanding of their own contexts, teachers' professionalism and the broader influences involved in making judgements about learning.

Pedagogy

Primary education as personal development would also demand an interrogation of the nature of pedagogy beyond teaching methods and the selective transfer of technical practices that appear to be effective in educational systems outside the UK. Wrigley *et al* (2012, 10) reject pedagogy as curriculum or assessment and suggest it is rather:

> 'the need for alignment between knowledge, curriculum, assessment, institutional mores and social context framed by understandings about the nature of knowledge, of reality and

human society, of human capacity for learning and growth and of aspiration for a better future.'

This definition has significant implications for an alternative view of primary education. It demands an evaluation of power relations in educational structures and professional relationships between staff; between teachers, children and families; the school, the classroom and local community. It has implications for the links between children's 'funds of knowledge' from home and school learning, and for the architecture and design of spaces where teaching and learning take place.

The introduction of competition as part of the neoliberal free market strategy for education, has no place in this definition of pedagogy. Currently, schools are in competition with each other for pupils and parents and university education departments are in competition for students. With the introduction of payment by results, teachers in the same school may soon be in competition with each other too. The business model does not translate to human learning. Teaching and learning are collaborative enterprises and teachers as well as children learn from each other. In the past teacher networks have provided strength and facilitated shared professional development as teachers have learnt from and supported each other in a spirit of partnership, rather than as passive recipients in courses about the requirements of the next national initiative.

Reframing primary education would also demand reform of initial teacher education, which since 1998 has been subject to centralised control, in many ways corresponding to that imposed upon schools. A well publicised government disdain for educational research and the denouncement of teacher educators as subversive Marxists

(Hall 2004) have been used to publicly justify centrally imposed direction. The detail of the curriculum and assessment framework for ITE is prescribed within a standards agenda that requires regulation by government agencies and surveillance by inspection, with punitive repercussions for institutions not considered to be 'compliant'. Recent policy implemented by Gove, creates a confusing array of routes to Qualified Teacher Status and confers responsibility for ITE on schools, in some cases excluding the involvement of higher education institutions; a move in the direction of privatisation as academy chains and others take over the role of teacher educators.

A view of education as development would necessitate beginning primary teachers learn more than the mechanics of teaching and have sufficient time and opportunity in universities to reflect critically on theory and research evidence. Relating their developing understanding of theory to the realities of the classroom will encourage new teachers to develop a philosophy of education, a set of principles upon which to build their future practice, and a basis from which to analyse and question policy.

After the Coalition, an alternative model of education as preparation for participation in a just society has the potential to transform primary schooling, if accompanied by the cultural and structural, and curricular changes outlined above, including a return to a democratically administered education system. Forming an alliance of teachers, support staff, parents, children, school leaders, academics, employers, and others to share their vision and assert their demands for education taking account of the lessons of history, will be the most positive and productive way forward for developing policy.

References

Ajegbo, K. (2007) *Diversity and Citizenship*. Nottingham: DfES.

Alexander, R. J. ed. (2010) *Children, their World, their Education. Final report and recommendations of the Cambridge Primary Review*. London: Routledge.

Chapman, J. & Chorley, M. (2013) 'A generation of unruly toddlers: Minister under-fire for "ill-judged" claims that nursery children aren't taught manners.' *Daily Mail online* 21.04.2013. http://www.dailymail.co.uk/news/article-2312657/A-generation-unruly-toddlers- html. Accessed 10.08.13

Charter for Primary Education (2013) http://primarycharter.files.wordpress.com/2013/03/primary-charter.pdf. Accessed 15.08.13.

Child Poverty Action Group. *Child Poverty Facts & Figures*. http://www.cpag.org.uk/child-poverty-facts-and-figures. Accessed 20.08.13

Department for Education (2013) *Primary Assessment and Accountability under the New National Curriculum*. London: HMSO.

Department for Education (2010) *The Importance of Teaching*. London: HMSO.

Department for Education and Skills (2004) *Every Child Matters: Change for Children*. London: HMSO.

Department for Education and Skills (2003) *Excellence and Enjoyment. A Strategy for Primary Schools.* London: HMSO.

Department of Education and Science (1975) *A Language for Life* (The Bullock Report). London: HMSO.

Department of Education and Science (1967) *Children and Their Primary Schools.* (The Plowden Report). London: HMSO.

Dombey, D. (2011) 'Panic About the Teaching of Reading'. *Books for Keeps.* January 2011.

Drummond, M.J. (2010) 'BRAVO! And BUT.... reading the Cambridge Primary Review'. *Forum* 52:1, 9-15.

Galton, M., Simon, B. & Croll, P.(1980) *Inside the Primary Classroom.* London: Routledge & Kegan Paul.

Gove, M. (2013) 'I refuse to surrender to the Marxist teachers hell-bent on destroying our schools'. http://www.dailymail.co.uk/debate/article-2298146/I-refuse-surrender-Marxist-teachers-html. *Mail Online.* Accessed 18.07.13.

Hall, K. (2004) *Literacy and Schooling. Towards Renewal in Primary Education Policy.* Aldershot: Ashgate.

Harlen,W. (2007) *The Quality of Learning : Assessment alternatives for primary education* (Primary Review Research Survey 3 / 4). Cambridge: University of Cambridge Faculty of Education.

Hart, S., Dixon, A., Drummond, M.J. & McIntyre, D. (2004) *Learning without Limits.* Maidenhead: Open University Press.

Kelly, C. (2010) *Hidden Worlds. Young Children Learning Literacy in Multicultural Contexts.* Stoke on Trent: Trentham.

Levin, B. (2013) *What Does It Take To Scale Up Innovations? An examination of Teach for America, the Harlem Children's Zone and the Knowledge is Power program.* nepc.colorado.edu/publication/scaling-up-innovation. Accessed 10.07.13

Ofsted (2013) *Unseen children.* Speech by Michael Wilshaw, Church House, Westminster, 20.06.2013. http://www.ofsted.gov.uk/resources/unseen-children-hmci-speech. Accessed 10.08.2013

O'Sullivan, O. & McGonigle, S. (2010) 'Transforming readers: teachers and children in the Centre for Literacy in Primary Education's Power of Reading project'. *Literacy* 44:2, 51-59.

Pollard, A., Broadfoot, P., Croll, P., Osborn, M., & Abbott, D. (1994) *Changing English Primary Schools? The Impact of the Education Reform Act at Key Stage 1.* London Cassell.

Ravitch, D. (2010) *The Death and Life of the Great American School System. How Testing and Choice Are Undermining Education.* New York: Basic Books.

Richards, C. (2010) 'A possible accountability framework for Primary Education: building on (but going beyond) the recommendations'. *Forum* 52:1, 37- 41.

Riley, K.A. (2013) 'Walking the leadership tightrope: building community cohesiveness and social capital in schools in highly disadvantaged urban communities'. *British Educational Research Journal* 39:2, 266 -286.

Thomas,W. & Collier, V. (1997) *Effectiveness for Language Minority Students.* Washington DC: National Clearinghouse for Bilingual Education.

Twist, L., Sizmur, J., Bartlet, S. & Lynn, L. (2012) PIRLS 2011: *Reading Achievement in England.* Research Report. NfER.

Warwick, P. (2008) 'Hearing pupils' voices: Revealing the need for citizenship education within primary schools'. *Education 3-13,* 34:1, 27-36.

Wrigley, T., Thomson, P. & Lingard, B. (2012) *Changing Schools. Alternative Ways To Make A Difference.* London: Routledge.

Wyse, D., McCreery, E. and Torrance, H. (2008) *The Trajectory and Impact of National Reform: Curriculum and assessment in English primary schools* (Primary Review Research Survey 3/2). Cambridge: University of Cambridge Faculty of Education.

Wyse, D. & Styles, M. (2007) 'Synthetic phonics and the teaching of reading: the debate surrounding England's "Rose Report"'. *Literacy* 41:1, 35-42.

.

Chapter 3

English for the Few or English for the Many?

Valerie Coultas

Introduction

There is nothing very new in Michael Gove's culturally elitist attitudes to English teaching and the comprehensive ideal. He joins a long line of those who have always been opposed to the basic principles of comprehensive education and democratic ideas about language and learning.

As Akpenye (2013) makes clear, the campaign against the comprehensive ideal has always been virulent. The 'child centred approach' to English teaching in comprehensive schools has come under particular attack. As long ago as 1969 a group of Conservative thinkers wrote a series of pamphlets, known as the Black Papers, that hit back hard against the key elements of what, for example, John Marenbon (1987,1994) dubbed 'the new orthodoxy'. The ideas in these papers constituted a full frontal attack on the ideas of progressive education and child-centred English teachers who, they suggested, were too concerned with ideas of personal growth. Instead, this group of Conservative thinkers argued that English was about teaching a body of knowledge, which involved re-establishing the pre-eminence of the English Literary Heritage and the explicit teaching of grammar and Standard English. They also began to establish the importance of

46

'standards' by arguing that standards would only be maintained in schools if they were clearly and publicly defined, hence the need for tests and league tables. These ideas influenced both major political parties and began to put Labour on the defensive in relation to comprehensive ideals.

The Coalition's educational polices stand on the shoulders of this attack on the comprehensive ideal and in this article I will identify some themes of the right's counter offensive against inclusive approaches to English teaching, explore some of the limitations of these ideas and begin to suggest how English might be promoted as a subject for all.

The pre-eminence of the English Literary Heritage

The over arching priority given to the English Literary Heritage or the canon is a key feature in this debate. In the new English curriculum (2013), secondary school pupils will have to study two plays by Shakespeare, Romantic poetry, a 19th century novel, First World War poets, post-war poetry and some world literature. This literary diet of 'dead, white men' has been described as 'impoverished' and 'too narrow' by the National Association for the Teaching of English (Garner 2013). One NATE member suggested that while 'it was good that we had a curriculum for a new century – it's just a shame it's the 19th and not the 21st' (Garner, *ibid*). NATE has argued that a wider range of contemporary literature and multi-modal texts should have been included.

Gove has justified his prescriptive approach on strongly nationalistic and conservative grounds:

'Our literature is the best in the world... It is every child's birthright and we should be proud to teach it in every school.' (2010, 41)

Such a dogmatic assertion implies a vast knowledge of world literature that he can surely not possess. It involves a dismissive attitude to literature from a wide range of cultures. It fails to acknowledge that many of the accepted great 'classics' of late nineteenth and twentieth century literature include works by, for example, Irish writers e.g. Yeats, Joyce, Wilde, Heaney. The new curriculum also marginalises the new multi-modal literacies that are at the centre of modern literacy practices. English Literature in the new GCSE is also in danger of once again becoming an option only for the top sets in state schools as the texts studied and the exam at the end will make some schools shy away from a whole cohort entry. White (2010) argues that Gove has an essentially rigid rather than a rigorous approach to the curriculum and that he is opposed to interdisciplinary collaboration and to areas that he conceives of as 'soft' knowledge, such as Media Studies.

The recitation of poetry is also given pride of place in the new English curriculum and, while the recitation or choric reading of a particular poem may be appropriate on some occasions, the overarching priority given to this 'puts pressure on teachers to rely on rote learning without understanding' (Bassey *et al* 2013).

A fixation with phonics as a panacea
When it comes to the teaching of Early Reading, rote learning is at the forefront as systematic synthetic phonics we are told is the most efficient way of delivering the 'alphabetic principle' (Rosen 2012). The screening test imposed on children at five includes non-words to assess their decoding skills. This extremely narrow approach, as

Mansell (2013) suggests, strongly promoted by those such as Ruth Miskin who have a financial interest in its success, is highly controversial and contested by many with expertise in the teaching of reading. Rosen (*ibid*) makes the point that the alphabetic principle is very difficult to sustain as the only principle in the teaching of reading as there are so many 'tricky words' that are in common use that do not adhere to this principle. Yet the new *Teachers Standards* (2012) are very explicit about how teachers must teach reading:

> 'A teacher must... If teaching early reading, demonstrate a clear understanding of systematic synthetic phonics;'

This contrasts starkly with what a teacher of early mathematics must do, which is 'demonstrate a clear understanding of appropriate strategies'. So Maths teachers have some opportunity to make some professional judgements about which approaches they should use but English teachers do not.

Again, we see how rigid the restrictions are on English teachers' pedagogy and pupils' learning. As Richmond (2013, 5) suggests 'the government is fixated on one and only one methodology, and is determined to impose its will'. (p5). He also refers to the role of New Labour in paving the way for this with its 'monomaniac zeal for phonics as strong as its Conservative predecessor' (Richmond 2013, 21).

Grammar - what big teeth you have?
The absolute importance given to the secretarial aspects of English such as grammar, punctuation and spelling as skills to be taught, learnt and tested at Key Stage 2, separately from their use in a piece of writing is another feature of this new curriculum (DfE 2013). This explains the new Key Stage Two grammar test where

skills in these areas are to be policed with rigour (Gove 2013). The new Key Stage Two Grammar test that pupils will take at 11 consists of decontextualized grammar exercises and multiple choice questions. Again, this links closely to the themes of the Black Paper writers who insisted that a body of knowledge must be established in English and that it must include grammar, punctuation and spelling (Jones 1989). The insistence on the separate testing of these secretarial skills again puts pressure on teachers to prepare pupils for the test in a decontextualized manner as the school's results will appear in the league tables and define the 'success' or 'failure' of the school in future inspections. The league tables will thus impel Senior Managers in Primary schools to conform to the new curriculum and prepare their pupils to perform well in this test of the secretarial aspects of English.

It must also be remembered that New Labour's National Literacy Strategy (DfES 1998) attempted to impose a form of teaching that lent credibility to the view that the secretarial aspects of 'Literacy', defined as reading and writing, were as – if not more – important than composition and meaning. Harshly critical of the whole language approach of the previous era that used pupils' life experiences and tacit knowledge of how language works as a stimulus for language development and writing, the NLS materials downgraded speaking and listening and focused on the deconstruction and analysis of the grammar of the text. New Labour's drive on literacy standards thus laid the groundwork for Gove's even sharper attack on progressive and inclusive approaches to English teaching (Coultas 2007, Coultas 2012).

Standard English

Another clear example of the elitism of the new Curriculum's approach to knowledge is the way in which the model of spoken language is changed in the new Curriculum (Coultas 2012). The *Teachers Standards* (2012) instruct teachers 'to take responsibility for... the correct use of Standard English whatever the teacher's specialist subject'.

The new English Curriculum (DfE 2013 a) has outlawed the speaking and listening strand and the new English language GCSE (DfE 2013b, 6) specifies that: 'Spoken language will be reported on as part of the qualification, but it will not form part of the final mark and grade'. The emphasis throughout the new curriculum is on the use of formal language, presentational talk and the use of spoken Standard English, imposing a passive and traditional view of the learner's spoken English. As others have noted, not only speaking and listening but also 'drama and modern media have almost disappeared from English...' (Bassey *et al ibid*).

This new 'cultural restorationist' (Jones 1989) Coalition English Curriculum represents a decisive break from the talk for learning model with regard to speaking and listening. It purposely puts Standard English on a pedestal 'as the language of knowledge' but obscures its class basis (Jones 1989, 69). This view is elitist because it directly contradicts the view expressed in the Bullock Report (1975) that pupils should not have to leave the language of the home behind them when they enter the classroom (Coultas 2012). While pupils should have opportunities to use standard and non-standard English, the new curriculum instructs teachers to promote the use of Standard English even in informal classroom conversations (DfE 2013a). It therefore seeks to turn the clock back on democratic views of spoken language development that highlighted the importance of informal talk, dialogue and classroom conversations (Barnes 2008). Such a retrograde view could encourage teachers to start 'correcting' pupils' spoken language and humiliate pupils who use colloquial language or non-standard dialects as happened in the past.

In a recent focus group discussion on oracy and dialogue in classrooms (Coultas 2013), the teachers felt that the dual nature of classroom talk, where as pupils learn to talk more effectively they should be also be talking to learn more effectively, was not fully understood. In the case of coalition Education policy, they thought the talk for learning model was under direct attack and that even the word 'oracy' was vanishing from the vocabulary of teachers.

A return to a one shot view of writing

By abolishing coursework and imposing a written exam at the end of the course the new Curriculum returns to the one shot view of writing, where the only writing that will count is that written under pressure in an unprepared exam. Real writers collaborate with others to share ideas and get feedback before they publish. The Process Approach to writing (Graves 1983) recognised this and allowed children to compose, draft and reflect on their writing. This view of the writer has informed the way English teachers teach children to write and written coursework allowed pupils to refine and enhance their writing skills as they used talk to compose writing and gain feedback on first drafts and then redraft. This led, in the 100% coursework era, to pupils producing a folder with a wide range of fiction and non-fiction forms of writing. This coincided with the natural development of the writer as many pupils begin to mature as writers at Key Stage four.

A deficit view of working-class culture and knowledge

These elitist themes in the New English curriculum are linked to a wider philosophy that views working-class culture, linguistic practices and knowledge as a deficit. This philosophy is also sceptical about educational theory and dismissive of ideas that link educational practices to child development. By caricaturing progressive educational ideas in headline grabbing and simplistic ways Gove seeks to re-establish meritocratic values that preserve elitism. For example, he deliberately and crudely counter-poses the acquisition of knowledge to a child-centred approach to teaching:

> 'Progressive educational theory stressed the importance of children following their own instincts *rather than being taught'* (Gove 2013, 3, my italics)

Yet at the heart of the new ideas about language and learning that developed in the '60s and '70s (Barnes *et al* 1969) was the need to link the new abstract ideas of the subject to the pupils own experiences and understanding. For as Barnes (1976) argued:

> 'Our pupils will learn most by reading, writing and talking about the experiences they meet and through *this in time will some to terms with subject knowledge.*' (126 my italics)

Not only did the new progressive language and learning approach require more skilful and sophisticated teaching techniques by the teacher, by using the social situation more effectively to set up small group learning and dialogue (Barnes 2008), but this approach also allows pupils to contest and interrogate knowledge itself rather than treating knowledge as a fixed and unchanging entity.

English for the many

Teachers will need to use the power they have in the classroom to continue to identify new collective ways forward that challenge retrograde approaches and go 'beyond the false certainties of performativity' (Clandinen 2012). The role of the teacher has some continuity and agency over different periods and phases for promoting English for all. As Amanda Coffey suggests, while

> 'the world of the teacher has changed... the everyday realities of the classroom have considerable similarities with the past.' (2001, 88)

Teaching, she suggests, will always be concerned with social practices and interactions in the classroom. Despite the many obstacles in the current context, the teacher or the department is still capable of mediating the curriculum and interpreting it in different ways (Kress *et al* 2005). I will now consider how English might be defended as a subject for the many in relation to the themes highlighted in this article.

Canonical and non-canonical texts

English teachers have always embraced canonical and non-canonical literature. Long before there was a National Curriculum teachers chose to teach Shakespeare and other pre-twentieth century texts and found ways to connect these texts with the lives and experiences of the pupils they taught: through drama, discussion and comparison with film and stage versions of the texts (Coultas 2009). But there was also an attempt to find modern and new literature that could stimulate new thoughts and discussion. Among these texts were those that more directly resonated with the experiences of contemporary pupils in multicultural Britain and we should continue to research and use the widest range of literature and texts in classrooms (*Collaborative Learning* 2011).

Reading as a meaning making process

We also have to insist that learning to read is a meaning making process. As John Richmond suggests, this is the big question about reading. When it comes to reading, young children

'learn to read by being introduced to and then recognising and remembering whole words in contexts that make sense, drawing on their existing understanding of those words in the spoken language.' (2013, 120)

He also outlines the other cues and prompts that assist children in making sense of print, for example: semantic, syntactic, phonetic, visual cues, bibliographic and textual cues. He points out that recent reports from Ofsted on reading bemoan the lack of reading policies in schools and

'the loss of once popular and effective strategies such as reading stories to younger children, listening to children read, and the sharing of complete novels with junior age children.'

Defending a balanced approach, where phonics is blended with other strategies, he argues that young children must learn that

'reading… is one of the principal sources of pleasure… indeed of joy and delight… that life affords.' (29)

Grammar is also about making meaning

The debate on grammar has never been about whether it should be taught but how it should be taught. Every time an English teacher marks a piece of work they comment first on the content of the writing but also on the secretarial aspects of English. But when it comes to teaching grammar directly, it's so much more effective to teach grammar in context, allowing pupils to use words and phrases in their own sentences and speech before parts are named. If you play I spy with a group and begin to emphasise the prepositions by speaking them aloud, the pupils begin to understand the role of that *part of speech* in the sentence. They begin to understand how the word works in a context. They are drawing on their own understandings and their own vocabulary to make meaning and then, when their understanding is more secure, they can give that word or phrase a name. Grammar cannot be truly understood as a technical list of terms, as a naming of parts, it has to be part of our tacit knowledge as we use language to communicate and make sense of the world around us.

Real writers collaborate

When it comes to writing, it is widely established that real writers draft and re-draft and that they often start from thoughts, observations and diary entries to express themselves and begin to compose ideas. This is because the crucial first question faced by any writer at any age is what do I want to say? Established writers then begin to write and often re-read and re-write their work for their chosen audience. English exams in the progressive era attempted to work with this process approach and English teachers will need to continue to create opportunities for this kind of practice as it is the best way of teaching all children to write with greater confidence.

Democratic education and equal societies

But, of course, curriculum and policy will need to change and in a true and inclusive English Baccalauriate or Diploma, taken at 17 or 18. English, a wide range of Literature, Drama and Media will need to play an essential part. Forms of assessment that allow pupils to show what they can do and that are relevant for the modern world must include oral skills and multi-modal forms as well as more traditional written forms as these are the literate tools that will be needed in the 21st century.

The comprehensive ideal, despite its critics, has been immensely powerful. Even Michael Gove tries to dress his elitist arguments up in terms of equal opportunities to access privileged and traditional knowledge. The bipartisanship of the two major parties on schooling must end. A progressive alliance needs to be re-established that defends the comprehensive principle and democratic and modern ideas about, for example, language in education much more rigorously and links this to the demand for greater equality in society as a whole. For, in more equal and democratic societies, the many not just the few are better educated.

References

Akpenye, G. (2013) 'The Comprehensive Ideal' in *Schools at Risk Gove's School Revolution Scrutinised. The reality behind the rhetoric. Essays on the current crisis*. London: SEA Publication.

Barnes, D. (1976) *From Communication to Curriculum*. Harmondsworth: Penguin.

Barnes, D. (2008) 'Exploratory Talk for Learning' in N. Mercer & E. Hodkinson (eds) *Exploratory Talk in School*. London: Sage, 1-17.

Barnes, D., Britton, J. & Rosen, H. (1969) *Language, the Learner and the School*. Harmondsworth: Penguin.

Bassey, M., Wrigley, T., Maguire, M., Pring, R., Goldstein, H. and 95 others (2013) letter to *The Independent*, Weds 20th May 2013.

Bullock, A. (1975) *A language for life: report of the Committee of Inquiry appointed by the Secretary of State for Education and Science under the chairman ship of Sir Allan Bullock.* London: HMSO.

Clandinen, J. (2012) *Speech to BERA Conference* September 15th 2013.

Coffey, A. (2001) *Education and Social Change.* Maidenhead: Open University Press.

Collaborative Learning Project (2011) http://www.collaborativelearning.org/firsttime.html accessed on June 15th 2011

Coultas, V. (2013) *What do teachers find challenging about classroom talk? A Critical Enquiry*, Draft PhD Thesis. London: Institute of Education.

Coultas, V. (2012) 'Let's Talk about Talk for Learning: Gove's Standards on Spoken English', *EnglishDramaMedia Magazine*, October, 58-60.

Coultas, V. (2009) 'Classic Texts, the Moving Image, Speaking and Listening and Pupils with EAL', *NALDIC Quarterly* 6 (3), 26-28.

Coultas, V. (2007) *Constructive Talk in Challenging Classrooms.* Oxford: Routledge.

Department for Education (2013a) *Programme of Study for English Key Stage Four* http://media.education.gov.uk/assets/files/pdf/e/english%20-%20key%20stage%204%2005-02-13.pdf , accessed July 26th 2013.

Department for Education (2013b) *GCSE English Language* http://media.education.gov.uk/assets/files/pdf/e/english%20-%20key%20stage%204%2005-0213.pdfhttps://www.gov.uk/government/uploads/system/uploads/attachment_data/file/206143/GCSE_English_Language_final.pdf accessed June 30th 2013.

Department for Education (2012) *Teachers' Standards* available at http://www.education.gov.uk/pubilcations/eOrderingDownload/teachers%20standardspdf accessed March 1st 2013.

Department for Education and Skills (1998) *The National Literacy Strategy Framework for Teaching*. London: DfES.

Garner, R. (2013) 'Pupils face literary diet of "dead white men"', *The Independent* 26th February 2013 available at http://www.independent.co.uk/news/education/education-news/pupils-face-literary-diet-of-dead-white-men

Gove, M. (2013) *The Progressive Betrayal*, speech to the Social Market Foundation, 5th February 2013, available at http://www.smf./co.uk/media/new/michael-gove-speaks.smf, accessed on 6th February 2013-09-06.

Gove, M. (2010) Speech to Conservative Party Conference October 5th 2010, available at http://blog.literaryconnections.co.uk/?p=550 accessed July 22nd 2011.

Graves, D. H. (1983) *Writing: Teachers and Children at Work*. Exeter: Heineman

Jones, K. (1989) *Right Turn, The Conservative Revolution in Education*. Hutchinson: Radius.

Kress, G., Jewitt, C., Bourne, J., Francis, A., Hardcastle, J., Jones, K . & Reid, E. (2005) *English in Urban Classrooms*. Abingdon: Routledge.

Mansell, W. (2012) 'The new national curriculum: made to order? New Questions are being asked about the framing of the primary curriculum', The Guardian 12th November 2012.

Marenbon, J. (1994) 'The new orthodoxy examined' in S. Brindley (ed) *Teaching English*, London: Routledge.

Marenbon, J. (1987) *English, Whose English?* London: Centre for Policy Studies.

Richmond, J. (2013) *Teaching Reading: How to.* London: United Kingdom Literacy Association.

Rosen, M. (2013) 'Letter from a Curious Parent', *The Guardian* June 13th 2012 available at www.ukla.org/news/stro/michael_rosens_letter_to_mr_gove_regarding_the_phonics_screening_test/ accessed on 22nd August 2012.

White, P. (2010) 'The Coalition and the Curriculum', *Forum* 52(3)

Chapter 4

Learning to Compete? Challenging Michael Gove's Fallacies on Standards and the Labour Market

Martin Allen

Introduction

Throughout Michael Gove's period as Secretary of State for Education there has been constant reference to the failure of education to respond to the economic challenges of the 21st century. In particular, 'falling standards' in schools have been seen as a major reason behind the UK's declining ability to 'compete' internationally and been used as justification for importing some of the features of more 'successful' systems – particularly those from the Pacific Rim.

Using the upper secondary years as an example, this chapter argues that changes to the examination system are being made for rather different reasons – part of a *Great Reversal* (Allen & Ainley 2013), an attempt to create a new correspondence between education and the declining employment opportunities for young people. The chapter also argues that developing alternatives to Gove's qualification examination reforms is an absolute priority but that action to address declining labour market opportunities is also necessary.

Michael Gove and *Reforming Key Stage Four*

Even though the 2012 GCSE grade crisis enabled him to promote examination reform on the wider political stage, Michael Gove had already set out clear intentions. The 2010 White Paper *The*

Importance of Teaching outlined proposals for an English Baccalaureate made up of a 'range of traditional subjects' and serving as a new basis for secondary school league tables (4.21). The White Paper also indicated that 'modules' would be replaced by linear courses with final exams – with changes to regulations about 'resits' (4.48). Meanwhile, Ofqual, the qualifications watchdog, had been given much greater influence, instructed to ensure that exam boards used a 'comparative outcomes' formula, reminiscent of the 'normative referencing' used in the old GCE O-levels. This effectively capped increases in pass rates from one year to another, thus precipitating the grade crisis that Gove cleverly sought to distance himself from.

Despite being forced to back-track on his proposals for replacing GCSE with English Baccalaureate Certificates (EBCs), Gove has ensured that the new GCSE requirements, published in June of this year, reflect his general priorities. Tiered papers are also being abolished and a new one to eight grading system being introduced, so as to differentiate higher level performance more clearly. Even if the EBC proposals have been shelved; the E-bacc subjects will feature prominently in the new Key Stage 4 league tables, making up five of the eight subjects through which schools will be ranked.

Though not receiving anywhere near the same attention, A-levels have been reformed in similar ways, with AS levels becoming stand-alone qualifications rather than a compulsory part of A-level taken at the end of the first year. With a clear intention of restoring A-level as a 'gold standard' qualification and the main entrance qualification for elite higher education, Gove has directed Russell universities to be directly involved in the determination of syllabus content. While universities like Cambridge and the LSE have published their own B lists of subjects considered less appropriate as entry qualifications, the Russells have now introduced 'facilitating' A-levels, effectively the E-bacc subjects from which applicants should study two.

While claiming to be introducing more 'rigour' in assessment, running through Gove's curriculum reforms has also been an emphasis on restoring the 'content' of learning. Signalling his intent while still in opposition, Gove told an RSA conference (30/06/09) that every citizen 'had the right to draw on our stock of intellectual capital', calling for more of an emphasis on 'hard facts'. Thus the White Paper referred to the importance of core knowledge in the traditional subjects 'that pupils should be expected to have to enable them to take their place as educated members of society' (4.9).

Gove himself has been influenced by US English Literature professor ED Hirsch. Hirsch argues that American schools have a 'knowledge deficit' – with many students, he argues, now being denied the things they need to know. Thus, the new GCSEs – some of which will begin in September 2014 – have clear content specifications, outlining very clearly what students should be taught. For example, 'at least one play by Shakespeare, at least one 19th century novel', to quote from the English Literature draft.

Gove has also sought to differentiate academic knowledge from practical, applied and vocational learning, publishing plans to prevent 'GCSE equivalent' vocational qualifications being counted in school league table scores on the grounds that these are much less demanding academically and require less curriculum time (White Paper, 4.51). More specifically, schools will not be able to include success in the current BTEC-style qualifications – reducing the status of these courses still further. To qualify for league table inclusion, vocational qualifications will need to be redesigned to look more like their academic counterparts, both in terms of their size and their assessment criteria. As a result, the number of vocational qualifications will be severely pruned.

Nevertheless, there have been disagreements between Conservatives over the role that vocational education plays at Key Stage 4. While the 2011 Wolf Review argued that students following vocational pathways were being 'short-changed' – in that these qualifications were 'valueless' in the labour market – Lord (Kenneth) Baker has continued to press ahead with University Technology Colleges (UTCs), providing specialist technical and vocational training from age 14 and enjoying support from Mike Tomlinson and Andrew Adonis.

Raising standards: restoring economic competitiveness and restarting social mobility?

What are the motives for Gove's reforms? Firstly, they are justified as responses to the 'dumbing down' of learning and to the exam 'grade inflation' which, he argues, took place under New Labour. Gove has made it clear that the new GCSEs will be more difficult to pass with Graham Stuart, chairman of the Parliamentary Select Committee on Education, arguing Gove could be paving the way for 'grade deflation' (*Independent 'I'* 16/06/13).

In *Reforming Key Stage Four*, the EBC consultation document, Gove cites an urgent need to restore 'public confidence' in an examinations system where '60% of those surveyed in a recent YouGov poll believe that GCSEs have got easier, while only 6% think that they have got harder' (3.4). More specifically:

> 'employers, universities and colleges are dissatisfied with school leavers' literacy and numeracy, with 42% of employers needing to organise additional training for at least some young people joining them from school or college'. (3.3)

Gove also frames his arguments in the context of what he considers to be the UK's declining international performance, looking to the education practices of high performing countries for inspiration. In other words, his concern about 'standards' is justifiable and necessary, he maintains, for the longer term ability of the UK economy to 'compete':

> '...the emphasis on effort is particularly marked in the Confucian-heritage countries such as China, Hong Kong SAR, Singapore, South Korea and Taiwan. The assumption here is that deep engagement with subject matter, including through memorisation where appropriate, leads to deeper understanding.' (8.6) and 'Hong Kong... as with South Korea and Singapore also operates with a curriculum model focusing on "fewer things in greater depth".' (White Paper 8.10)

This claim has continued unabated throughout Gove's offensive:

> 'There is clear evidence that the standards of our examinations have fallen over time and that the expectations they set for our students are now below those of our international competitors... New GCSEs will set expectations that match and exceed those in the highest performing jurisdictions.' (DfE, Reformed GCSE subject content consultation, June 2013).

Launching a new National Curriculum in July that requires five-year olds to calculate fractions and write computer programmes, Gove told ITV's *Daybreak* (08/07/13), 'I want my children, who are in primary school at the moment, to have the sort of curriculum that children in other countries have, which are doing better than our own'. This type of comparative analysis has always been highly selective (see Morris 2012) and compares very different traditions of education, including those requiring pictographic characters as opposed to phonic literacy (!). Even Sir Michael Barber, architect of many 'school improvement' reforms during the last two decades, has warned about the dangers of copying policy on the hoof (*Guardian* 22/8/12). Barber also pointed out that as policy makers in the Asian Tiger economies recognise that their economic systems need to become 'more innovative' and their schools 'more creative', some of the countries Gove admires are now looking to European education systems for inspiration.

Secondly, such comparisons have always been politically loaded. It is the rote learning and fact regurgitation of the Pacific Rim countries, rather than the relaxed and successful education system of league table free Finland (increasingly omitted from Gove's examples and a country with relatively low levels of 'school autonomy'), that have received attention. There are many other political, economic and social reasons for the high growth rates in the Pacific Rim that have little to do with their education programmes; for example, greater state involvement in investment plans, lower levels of wages and lack of labour market regulation and, in some cases, restrictions on trade unions.

Thirdly, as *The Guardian*'s Peter Wilby (08/12/2012) pointed out, the specific OECD international tests on which Gove based his evidence had since been declared invalid with officials reprimanded. For example, less than three months after Gove had published his proposals for exam reform, new 'global league tables' published by the multi-national education supplier Pearson and compiled by the Economist Intelligence Unit, ranked the UK sixth best in the world – although Finland and South Korea remained first and second. Oxford University researchers OUCEA (2013) have also argued that international test data as a whole cannot be taken at face value and are extremely limited ways of measuring a country's educational standards.

Gove's arguments about the need to return to a more 'knowledge based' curriculum deserve more serious attention. The need to 'bring knowledge back in' has for example, been endorsed by, amongst others, Michael Young (Young 2008) who was associated with the 'social constructionist 'curriculum in the 1970s and by no means a supporter of Gove or the Coalition. Gove's mentor Hirsch argues a lack of 'core knowledge' denies disadvantaged children the chance to move on in society (an inversion of Bourdieu's 'cultural capital' argument). Attempting to position himself as a leading advocate of 'social mobility', Gove's 'Blairite' credentials win praise from Labour right-winger Adonis, but also from Labour renegade, now *Telegraph* columnist and Free School promoter, Toby Young:

> 'Not so long ago, the labour movement put great emphasis on the acquisition of knowledge, with Left-wing intellectuals like R.H. Tawny believing all children should be introduced to the best that's been thought and said, regardless of background. How that philosophy came to be embraced by a Conservative, with Labour politicians defending the idea that the children of the poor should study the words of Simon Cowell rather than Shakespeare, is one of the great mysteries of the age'. (*Telegraph* 13/6/13)

Rather than calling for the reintroduction of grammar schools however, Adonis and Young unite behind Gove in his academies drive, Adonis seeing academies having the potential to recreate the ethos, traditions and curriculum of the grammars, but maintaining a 'comprehensive intake', thus ensuring social mobility. This argument that social mobility can be reignited, providing there is the right sort of learning in schools, has been reinforced by Ofsted

Chief Inspector of Schools, Michael Wilshaw (*Guardian*, 15/06/13 and BBC News.co.uk 21/06/13) and used to justify the government's academy programme.

A reactionary not a 'moderniser'

As will be argued below, reintroducing 'a grammar school curriculum for all' (Allen 2012) is not going to kick-start social mobility – just as re-establishing apprenticeships is not going to resurrect the 'technician mobility' of the post-war years (as Universities Minister Willetts argued on Radio 4, 24/06/13). On the contrary, Gove's curriculum project represents a step backwards, being used to narrow and to emphasize particular approaches to learning. For example, phonics and reading tests for young children in primary schools and requirements that children concentrate on memorising tables or particular types of mathematical calculations at the expense of other numeracy skills.

In subjects like history this also involves resurrecting particular conceptions of knowledge and 'nationhood'. For example, Gove considers the school history curriculum should reflect a particular heritage: 'I believe very strongly that education is about the transfer of knowledge from one generation to the next... The facts, dates and narrative of our history in fact join us all together.' (Westminster Academy speech quoted by Allen 2012) In his RSA speech, Gove similarly lamented the results of a survey in which many history students entering Russell universities named Nelson, rather than Wellington in charge at Waterloo. Thus, former-Coalition Schools Minister, Nick Gibb, promised that in future history syllabuses would prioritise the values of 'knowledge and scholarship' rather than 'enquiry' and 'interpretation'. Rather than an emphasis on 'how to learn about history', there needs to be an emphasis, he argued, on 'what history to learn' (*Telegraph* 22/10/12).

Far from promoting economic modernisation through education, Gove's 'Kings and Queens' history curriculum, even if, as a result of opposition from historians and teachers, he has been forced to make significant concessions, reflects the 'restorationist' agenda central to the Conservative project of the 1980s (Jones 1989). Wanting to reverse an epoch of pedagogic reform and wanting to restore traditional curriculum hierarchies at the expense of newer subjects, was exemplified in the idea of the Ebacc.

Young people and qualifications, a changing context

Rather than based on any real evidence, Gove's attempts to blame the examination system for falling standards, let alone the UK's declining ability to compete economically, are part of a determined attack on post-war comprehensive ideals. Replacing grammar schools with comprehensives made educational opportunities more equal and, in particular, replacing O-levels with GCSEs and more open forms of assessment, where students know what they have to do to reach a certain level, along with the extension of course work, has also been an important reason why performance levels have increased. Helped by the *Curriculum 2000* proposals, A-level entries and A-level passes have risen to unprecedented levels with one in four candidates now achieving an A grade.

Despite Gove claiming his arguments about falling standards and 'dumbing down' are backed by academic evidence (*Reforming Key Stage* 4, 3.4), it is not clear if research findings can ever be conclusive. Ofqual may consider multi-choice assessment less demanding than old-style essay writing (Allen and Ainley 2013) but they test different abilities under different conditions. The Oxford researchers referred to earlier, argue that evidence about modular assessment being easier is 'mixed' and that an end of course written exam may not be enough as a test of main knowledge and skills.

This is not to deny there have been issues. As a result of league table pressures, teachers have 'taught to the test', schools have given undue amounts of attention to some students rather than others and of course there has been a huge growth in commercial revision guides and tutorial services. If we are to reclaim the debate about 'standards', we have to understand that this issue is both a complex one, but also one that cannot be separated from wider social and economic changes. For example, in his Enquiry into the grading controversy surrounding the 2002 A-levels Professor Tomlinson concluded:

> 'I believe it to be vital that there is greater public understanding of the examination process and that as a consequence there is an end to the annual argument about results. The standard has not been lowered if an increased proportion of students meet it as a consequence of improved teaching and hard work.'

Tomlinson's comments illustrate the inherently insolvable tensions behind the debate about exam standards. Are standards really falling or is the problem that there are too many people meeting them and that as a result, particular qualifications are now less exclusive?

In post-war years qualifications were predominantly seen as requirements for white-collar employment and many working-class school leavers, especially boys without or with few qualifications, could make a relatively easy transition to industrial manual work, including apprenticeships. Now, with the decline in real employment opportunities, most will consider gaining the good exam grades essential as labour market labour currency to improve their place in the 'jobs queue' (Allen and Ainley 2013). In a slack labour market employers also know they can recruit well qualified (now 'overqualified') young people for jobs for which qualifications were not previously required. Thinking that social mobility can be restarted by returning to a grammar school curriculum without addressing employment opportunities is an illusion.

The fact that one in four jobs now require degrees (UKCES 2012), largely as screening for applicants, says as much about increases in the number of graduates, as it provides conclusive evidence of increases in skill requirements. According to the Higher Education Statistics Agency (2013), a third of graduates who had left university in 2012 and had found employment six months later were working in occupational groups that were not 'professional' and with almost one in ten unemployed.

As a result, it is the increased demand for qualifications by young people, including continuing demand for university places, despite the huge increases in fees, that provides as good an explanation for the so-called 'grade inflation' as changes in the content of learning and its assessment. For more and more young people, the education system is like running up a downwards escalator where you have to run faster simply to stand still.

In our book, *The Great Reversal,* Patrick Ainley and I argue that, rather than being something that promotes and improves individual aspiration and social mobility, Gove's curriculum proposals are part of a wider programme of reversing progressive reform in education. In 'a declining economy' social mobility has gone into reverse and cannot simply be restarted through education reforms. It was the expanding economy of the post-war period and the significant increase in managerial and professional jobs that allowed working-class children to move up the occupational structure, certainly not grammar schools providing access to particular forms of elite knowledge in the way that Gove, Adonis and Young imply.

New Labour also promoted illusionary ideas about the global economy providing 'more room at the top' but the reality is that the occupational structure is rather different to the one predicted by Blair and Brown. Instead, it is argued that it is becoming 'hour-glass shaped' (Lansley 2012) with new managerial and professional jobs being created but also a raft of new low-skilled jobs and the 'hollowing out' of the middle. Alternatively, the occupational structure can be seen as going 'pear-shaped' with, for example, professional work increasingly undertaken by 'para-professional' labour (Allen and Ainley 2013) with nowhere near enough well-paid jobs for those who are 'qualified' to do them.

Whatever the exact nature of the occupational structure, the extent of the 'mismatch' between the educational qualifications that young people hold and the employment opportunities is more than clear. Felstead and Green (2012) showed that in 2012 there were 1.5 million more people with level 4 or above certificates than there were jobs requiring this level of qualification for entry (let alone for their actual performance!). This is more than those requiring no qualifications on entry (UKCES 2012). But this tells us more about the number of graduates in the jobs queue than it does about the increased skill level of jobs. As more jobs become 'graduatised' (UKCES reporting an increase of 1.9 million graduate jobs between 2006 and 2012, alongside a corresponding increase in the number of graduates), the boundaries between graduate and non-graduate work become increasingly fuzzy.

As a result, further 'mismatch' occurs lower down with Felstead and Green also showing supply exceeded demand at level 3 (A-level or equivalent) by 2.5 million and at level 2 (GCSE or equivalent) by 2.2 million. As those with lower qualifications are bumped down the queue and the number of people in the labour market with no qualifications at all fell in 2012 to only 1.5 million, 5.9 million jobs require no qualifications. At the bottom end of the occupational structure there thus continues to be a strong correlation between unemployment and a lack of qualifications, but this is because of excess supply of labour as much as it is a decline in jobs. It is also a reason for what Wolf (2011) refers to as young people being 'pushed' back into full-time education to improve their relative advantage, rather than 'pulled' back because they don't have enough skills. According to the International Labour Organisation (ILO 2013), the 'overeducation' of young people is now more serious than a lack of qualifications (referred to as 'undereducation').

With huge increases in the number of degree holders however, the relative advantages of attending university (referred to as 'the graduate premium') not only cannot be guaranteed, but becomes increasingly risky with the danger of financial loss increasing if you 'fail' and fall below the new benchmark 2.1 that was previously only required for the further expense of post-graduate study. As Brynin (2013) recognises, arguments about the continued significance of the graduate premium take no account of issues about 'distribution' – some graduates enjoying a huge premium but others earning little more than non-graduates, sometimes even less. With a third of graduates within 'a pay band from 30% above and 30% below the mean', Brynin suggests that within 15 years about half of these are likely to be earning only an average income but that 'more and more school leavers have to become graduates in order to earn average pay' (290).

Though the graduate recruitment consultancy 'High Flyers' maintains there will be a slight improvement in graduate employment opportunities for 2013, (BBC News 13/01/13) the agency's prediction is restricted to the top 100 graduate employers. The Higher Education Statistics Agency figures provide a much bleaker picture, showing that 36% of graduates who left university in the last year were working in occupational groups classed as 'non-professional' – 13% in sales and customer services, – and almost one in ten out of work. HESA also reported a 'mean' graduate salary of £21,000 – the same level at which students are currently required to start paying back student loans – but a 'median' salary of £20,000.

A new correspondence for education and the labour market
The aim of the Gove school reforms are part of an attempt to create a new 'correspondence' between education and the economy in a situation of decreasing labour market opportunities. This involves state education returning to its traditional social control functions – explicit from the beginning in the 1870 Education Act. Rather than being a vehicle for social mobility and individual progression, educational opportunities are rationed by making exams harder but also, as with David Willetts' higher education reforms, progression to university is now a more precarious and more expensive activity. Complementing Gove's attempts to recreate a more exclusive academic education in schools, have been Willetts' efforts to limit the growth of, if not reduce the size of, the university sector by trebling tuition fees to £9,000. Willetts' hopes for a market in uni' fees have been undermined by the fact that most English institutions are charging the highest level. Even if there has been a dip in applications and, according to the Sutton Trust (2013), 'more than two-thirds of secondary school pupils in England and Wales have major reservations about the cost of going to university' initial evidence (or UCAS data at least) shows that young people may not be put off applying if they consider there are

no other opportunities and if, as argued, some form of 'graduate premium' continues to exist. They may also conclude that with average earnings falling in real terms, they may never have to pay off their student loans! In fact, it is the potential implications of a student debt bubble (McGettigan 2013) with two out of five debts in danger of not being repaid, that is now becoming a concern to the Treasury (*Sunday Time* 21/04/13), adding to pressure on Willetts and with the implication that loan interest rates may have to increase, or more significantly, the income threshold level after which the repayments kick-in having to be lowered.

Apprenticeships. Doing it the German way?

The flip-side to reducing the number of university students has been the rolling out of new apprenticeship programmes as the Coalition promised 250,000 more by 2015, following Wolf's report that work-based learning provides much higher returns than classroom-based vocational education. Those like Baker and Adonis, but also Will Hutton (*Observer,* 10/03/13), who look to the German model of apprenticeships as the way forward, will have been encouraged by Angela Merkel's comments about the success of the 'dual system' in not 'just trying to make our young people academic' *(Guardian,* 03/06/13). According to the IPPR (2013), while a smaller proportion of young people in Germany may attend university, a far greater number complete years-long apprenticeships with 90% of trainees securing proper employment. The German apprenticeship system however was a product of post-war 'social partnership', something which Merkel's neo-liberal policies are intended to reverse. Employers and trade unions established a national framework involving both legislation and much higher levels of state involvement and financing than the British 'market state' could possibly allow (as Hutton recognises). As a result, the German apprenticeship system, which stretches well beyond the manufacturing sector, means that many young people have only been legally allowed to enter many occupations when they have completed the apprenticeship programme supporting them. Nor can even small employers set up new businesses without taking on and training apprentices. Even so, for many years now, more young Germans follow the grammar school route to higher education than combine technical schooling with apprenticeship.

In the UK, where the industrial base has been largely replaced by an invariably low-skilled, poorly paid service sector, most employers simply don't need apprentices. Some employers have even used government funding to upgrade existing employees to apprentices; for example, 'apprenticeships' for those completing short-term training courses for supermarket work and many other schemes continue to be for less than six months, only offering low-level training and qualifications. According to the IPPR (2013) around 40% of 'apprenticeships' go to people over the age of 25 as starts for those aged over 25 increased by 234% between the middle of 2010 and the end of the first quarter of 2011

When employers do genuinely seek to recruit young people for apprenticeships linked to guaranteed future employment, applications massively outstrip vacancies with demand for places on the few legitimate schemes being in some cases up to ten times over-subscribed *(Independent* 30/05/2013). Rolls Royce schemes are notoriously harder to get into than Oxbridge. Once again, this confirms that youth unemployment is a job, not a skills problem, even if the two are often confused. A genuine apprenticeship system would need to be part of a longer-term economic regeneration and employment strategy. Neither Coalition nor Labour, for that matter, have one.

New Strategies for Youth and Education

New strategies are needed to ensure future economic security for young people that go well beyond the reform of education – although this is still both necessary and desirable.

First of all, there needs to be a series of alternative economic policies in the interests of the new generations and for the future of society. This would be part of a plan B(+) for the economy in general, accepting that without a 'Keynesian' fiscal stimulus there will be no serious reduction of unemployment. In this respect, Labour's commitment to continuing with Coalition spending targets effectively prevents a programme of state-funded job creation, which must be central to any alternative (Allen and Ainley 2013). Disappointingly, though offering job guarantees to young people who have been out of work for six months, current Labour Party thinking still fails to properly acknowledge the reality that young people face in the labour market. 'We have an education system which does not prepare people for work' (Labour Skills Taskforce Interim Report 2013); yet the same document also refers to findings from UKCES that only one in five employers actively try to recruit young people and of those who do, only one in four find them poorly prepared for the workplace and this mostly applied to graduates (Skills Taskforce 6). Other research (CIPD 2013) also shows few employers specifically target young people for recruitment, resulting in the job search process being a 'frustrating and demotivating experience' and highlighting the need for more youth friendly selection procedures, including reinstated careers guidance.

With Nick Clegg now admitting that the Coalition's £1bn 'Youth Contract' has done little to reduce the number of those Not in Education Employment or Training (NEET) (*Guardian* 16/07/13) and with research showing it just as expensive to keep a young person on the dole, a specific programme of youth job creation must build on but also go well beyond the last Labour government's Future Jobs Fund, which was based on much higher levels of employer subsidies but was also pitched towards public and voluntary sector organisations, rather than private business.

Local Authorities, providing they are given the power and finance to do so, can also work alongside voluntary organisations to provide more secure employment opportunities for young people (Ainley and Allen 2010). Here there are some encouraging signs that Labour is considering a more coordinated approach towards matching young people with potential employers, but without an alternative plan for the economy, these types of initiatives can only remain severely compromised.

A general diploma for everybody

Even if we cannot 'educate our way out of recession', Gove's reforms need to be challenged with a coherent alternative rather than just reverting to the status quo. While we do not need a new sheep and goats test at 16, neither do we need to prioritise an exclusively academic curriculum any more than we do the (often illusory) 'skills' of vocational learning. Bringing together current academic and vocational qualifications in a 'general diploma' within a core curriculum entitlement could be a start to this process.

But it would have to be the diploma as a whole, rather than these individual qualifications that would have to be recognised as the main achievement. This has been a potential tension in previous blueprints for reform, including the Tomlinson proposals (DfES 2004), where elite schools would have been able to pay lip service to the principles behind an overarching certificate but then continue with an exclusive curriculum offer. If the general diploma is to both allow for more specialisation by students as they get older, but also to act as a 'leveller', then, while it could be administered and developed through localised networks, a degree of central state intervention would be unavoidable.

With staying on in education already the norm, even before the official raising of the participation age, such a diploma, awarded at 18, with an intermediate level at 16, could also represent a stage in the transition to adulthood explicitly linked to the rights and responsibilities of citizenship. The general diploma should also be accessed by all to provide a mandatory entitlement to a range of learning, but also constitute the main avenue of progression to further, higher and adult continuing education and training.

Most importantly, reforming education and exams at Key Stage 4 should also be part of a more general debate about learning in the 21st century and the search for a post-Gove consensus.

References
Ainley, P. & Allen, M. (2010) *Lost Generation? New strategies for youth and education*. London: Continuum.

Allen, M. (2012) 'Back to the Grammar School' *Education for Liberation Issue 5* April 2012.
(http://radicaled.wordpress.com/2012/04/12/back-to-the-grammar-school/)

Allen, M. & Ainley, P. (2013) *The Great Reversal. Education and Employment in a Declining Economy*. London: Radicaled.

Brynin, M. (2013) 'Individual Choice and Risk: The case of Higher Education' *Sociology* 2013, 47. (http://soc.sagepub.com/)

Chartered Institute of Personnel Development (April 2013) *Employers are from Mars, Young People are from Venus: Addressing the Young People/Jobs Mismatch.* www.cipd.co.uk

Department for Education (2010) *The importance of Teaching.* London: HMSO.

Department for Education (2012) *Reforming Key Stage 4.* DfE.

Department for Education and Skills (2004) *14-19 Curriculum and Qualifications Reform*: final report of the working group on 14-19 reform. Nottingham: DfES.

Felstead, A. and Green, F. (2013) *Skills in Focus, Underutilization overqualification and skills mismatch: patterns and trends.* London: Joint Skills Committee.

Higher Education Statistics Agency (2013). (http://www.hesa.ac.uk/content/view/2903/393/)

International Labour Organisation (2013) *Global Employment Trends for Youth* (www.ilo.org).

Institute for Public Policy Research (2013) *Rethinking Apprenticeships* (www.ippr.org/publications/55/8028/rethinking-apprenticeships).

Jones, K. (1989) *Right Turn.* London: Hutchinson.

Labour Party (2013) *Taskforce Interim Report.*

Lansley, S. (2012) *The Cost of Inequality.* London: Gibson

McGettigan, A. (2013) *The Great University Robbery.* London: Pluto.

Morris, A. (2012) 'Pick 'n' mix, select and project; policy borrowing and the quest for "world class" schooling: an analysis of the 2010 schools White Paper,' *Journal of Education Policy*, 27.1.

Oxford University Centre for Educational research (2013) (http://oucea.education.ox.ac.uk/research/recent-research-projects/research-evidence-relating-to-proposals-for-reform-of-the-gcse/).

Sutton Trust (2013) Press release downloaded 13/05/2013 (www.suttontrust.com/news/news/two-thirds-of-11-16-year-olds-have-university-finance-fears/).

Tomlinson, M.(2002) *Enquiry into A-level standards,* DfES.

UK Commission for Employment and Skills (2012) *Skills at Work in Britain, First Findings from the Skills and Employment Survey.* London: UKCES.

Wolf, A. (2011) *Review of Vocational Education. The Wolf Report.* London: *Department* for Education.

Young, M. (2008) *Bringing Knowledge Back In. From social constructivism to social realism in the sociology of education.* London: Routledge.

Chapter 5

'Sorry to have kept you waiting so long, Mr. Macfarlane': Further Education after the Coalition

Robin Simmons

Introduction

This chapter focuses on the further education (FE) sector, a part of the education system – if indeed system is the correct term – which has suffered more than most under the Coalition. Although FE has always been something of a 'Cinderella service', savage funding cuts and far-reaching systemic changes mean that its prospects now look particularly bleak. Drawing on recommendations made in the first draft of the often forgotten Macfarlane Report of 1980, I set out a radically different future for further education: a future in which the muddled and incoherent FE sector we see today is transformed into national system of tertiary colleges – organisations which would be at the centre of a greatly simplified system of comprehensive post-school education and training. Before planning the future it is, however, necessary to understand the present and so, initially, I provide an overview of the FE sector and explain how it has arrived at its current condition. The chapter therefore first provides a brief overview of the history of further education and summarises some of the main characteristics of the Coalition's approach to FE before turning to the future of further education.

Further education in England: a brief history

In England the FE sector is made up of a diverse range of providers including sixth-form colleges, school sixth forms and what remains of adult education services run by local authorities. Specialist colleges catering for subjects such as art and design, agriculture, and performing arts also exist. Other institutions serve particular groups of students such as adult returners or learners with special educational needs. Private and voluntary providers are an important part of the landscape: since the 1980s, successive governments have driven the commercialisation and marketization of post-compulsory education and training, and today the English further education sector is effectively a 'mixed-economy' of public sector providers competing with each other and literally thousands of voluntary and private sector organisations. FE is therefore complicated and difficult to understand, not only for those with little direct experience of the sector but also for many working or studying within it (Orr and Simmons 2010). Whilst there are some significant differences in the different nations of the UK – in Scotland, for example, sixth-form colleges do not exist and private providers play a less significant role than in England – in each nation general FE colleges are the largest and most 'weighty' providers of further education.

FE colleges offer a broad and diverse variety of learning opportunities, ranging from courses for people with learning difficulties through to degree-level programmes. In some ways FE also overlaps with the work of schools, both in terms of competition for young people over the age of 16 and with regard to collaborative provision for 14-16 year olds thought more suitable for vocational or work-related education rather than academic study. Introductory and intermediate vocational learning for those above the minimum school-leaving age has, however, always been further education's 'core business' and most FE courses focus on teaching the skills and knowledge needed for everyday employment – whether this is on the construction site, in the engineering workshop, the care home, office or hotel. Basically, further education has always been about education and training for working-class people and consequently few policymakers have direct experience of FE: in class-conscious England, further education colleges have always been better suited to 'other people's children' (Richardson 2007, 411).

The origins of some of today's FE colleges can be traced back to the mechanics institutes of nineteenth century England but local education authorities (LEAs) played a key role in their development. However, municipal involvement was initially voluntary and so many parts of the country, including some of its major industrial towns and cities were left without meaningful provision (Bailey 1987, 52-55). Later, there was a huge growth of further education after the 1944 Education Act placed a statutory duty on all LEAs to provide 'adequate facilities' for FE. The notion of adequacy is, of course, open to interpretation and the way in which each local authority carried out its responsibilities depended, to a great extent, on what Waitt (1980, 402) describes as a 'local ecology'. One important feature of this was the variable level of finance different LEAs awarded to different colleges across the country. The size, remit and ethos of each college were also shaped, at least in part, by the presence (or absence) of local schools, polytechnics and universities, as well as by other colleges. Moreover, some local authorities allowed colleges considerable autonomy in their affairs whilst others were, at their worst, stifling and restrictive (Waitt 1980, 397-402). One way of describing FE under local authority control is that it was 'variable' – and that this variability existed at a number of different levels: between different authorities; within different authorities; and even between different departments within individual colleges (Simmons 2008, 361). More bluntly, Ainley and Bailey (1997, 103) describe the era of LEA control as 'a mishmash of brilliance... and diabolical practice'.

Whatever arrangements local authorities made, for three decades after the end of World War Two FE colleges were basically locally-run organisations on the margins of the education system (Lucas 2004, 36-8). This situation began to change as increasing disquiet about the performance of the education system began to be voiced. Although predated by the 'Black Papers' and other, mainly Right-wing critiques, James Callaghan's (1976) 'Great Debate' speech infamously linked the UK's relative economic decline with the perceived inability of schools and colleges to produce enough 'employable' young people. Thereafter successive governments intensified such criticisms and championed the need for greater efficiency and responsiveness to consumer needs. Teachers, like other public servants, were viewed as protected from the rigours of competition through excessive trade union power, weak management and overly generous terms and conditions. Gravatt and Silver's (2000, 116-117) critique of FE under local authority control encapsulates many of the criticisms made about the public services at the time – that parochialism, inefficiency and 'vested interests' dominated at the expense of consumer needs. One would not, however, need to be a zealous neo-liberal to object to some of the traditions and practices that characterised the 'golden years' of LEA control. Whilst, officially, local authorities were accountable through the democratic process, the reality was often rather different. Decision-making could be slow and some LEAs were not particularly open to change (Simmons 2008). Historically, most colleges were dominated by certain relatively privileged sections of the working class and there was sometimes a reluctance to engage with the needs of 'non-traditional' users such as women, ethnic minorities or mature students (FEU 1979).

During the 1980s, public utilities and nationalised industries were incrementally privatised but more politically sensitive public services such as education could not so easily be sold off. A combination of quasi-market forces and strict limits on public expenditure was used in order to reproduce the conditions of the private sector instead. At the same time, there was increasing state intervention in the education system and a series of legislative changes which aimed to re-direct education in order to serve the perceived needs of the economy. The 1988 Education Reform Act focused mainly on schools but also resulted in important changes in the way FE was financed and governed. The 1992 Further and Higher Education was, however, pivotal for further education and, following this Act, all FE colleges were removed from LEA control – a process known as 'incorporation'. Each institution became fully responsible for its own affairs; principals became 'chief executives'; and colleges were required to compete against each other, schools, universities and other education and training providers in marketized conditions engineered and maintained by the state (Simmons 2008, 359). Arguably, the decline of the UK's traditional industrial base and broader social change meant it was necessary to remove colleges from municipal control to allow them to operate more flexibly in a changing environment, but the particular form which incorporation took was closely associated with neo-liberalism (Simmons 2010, 366). Following incorporation, 20,000 staff left FE through redundancies, early retirement and ill-health (Burchill 1998). Cumulative reductions in funding meant that the amount colleges received per full-time equivalent student was reduced by over 20% in the first five years of incorporation (FEFC 1998). Pay and conditions deteriorated and teachers' professional autonomy was significantly curtailed; macho-management, strike action and industrial unrest became commonplace. FE colleges became far more taxing places in which to work, particularly for teaching staff (Randle and Brady 1997).

Although there is no doubt that FE was in a state of disarray when New Labour came to power in 1997, it must also be noted that many colleges became more open and outward-looking after incorporation. FE embraced new areas of work, engaged with new constituencies of students, and, in some ways, colleges were forced to operate in a more transparent fashion than had been the case hitherto. But whilst there were certain continuities between New Labour and its Conservative predecessors (Hodgson and Spours 2006), the governments of Blair and Brown were less overtly aggressive towards FE. There was, however, much rhetoric about 'up-skilling' and further education's supposed role in creating a 'knowledge economy'. New Labour's vision was that FE was the key to both economic success and social justice (Cabinet Office 2008) and, from 2001 onwards, colleges were provided with substantially increased funding – much of which manifested itself in improved facilities and shiny new buildings. The *quid pro quo* was an avalanche of interventions and policy initiatives, the extent of which lead Frank Coffield (2006, 18-19) to describe FE under New Labour as a sector dominated by diktat and discipline, performativity and managerialism.

The Coalition and Further Education
There are significant similarities between the Coalition's approach to further education and that of New Labour – both, for example, valorise 'skills' and see market competition as the best way to improve the sector (Avis 2011). There are, however, also important differences between their approaches, one of which is the

peculiarly utilitarian and old-fashioned conception of vocational learning evident amongst key figures within the Coalition's Conservative leadership (Fisher and Simmons 2012, 41). Whilst the introduction of compulsory teacher training for FE teachers was an important part of New Labour's drive to 'professionalise' the sector, Coalition policymakers display a marked antipathy towards formal teacher training in general and for FE teachers in particular. The recent decision to rescind the statutory requirement for teaching staff in colleges to hold formal teaching qualifications is consistent with the essentially liberal values which underpin the Coalition's education policy.

> '...staff training, professional updating, competency and behaviour are essentially matters between employer and employee. There are sufficient statutory arrangements in place through, for example, employment legislation and the requirements for staff performance management and learner safeguarding set out in Ofsted's *Common Inspection Framework*, to ensure at least a threshold level of professional performance.' (DBIS 2012, 6)

The decision to end compulsory teacher training for FE teachers is, however, also rooted in a particular conception of teaching as essentially a skills-based 'craft' as opposed to a professional practice (see, for example, Gove 2010). Whilst this is evident in the way senior Coalition figures regard teaching in general, their conception of FE teaching draws on a combination of romance and condescension to promote old-fashioned images of technical instruction as opposed to broader forms of pedagogy rooted in a body of principled knowledge.

Another difference between the two governments' approach to FE is, of course, the Coalition's regime of extreme cost-cutting which has, so far, included scrapping the Educational Maintenance Allowance for 16-18 year olds; removing all public funding for those studying level 3 courses over the age of 24; ending the entitlement for people over the age of 25 to take a first level 2 qualification free of charge; and pulling the plug on various college building projects. All this is set against overall reductions in funding of over 25%, on-going programmes of restructuring, redundancies, and a culture of 'more for less' across the FE sector. Deep funding cuts have, however, been accompanied by a discourse of freedom. Speaking at the Association of College's Annual Conference shortly before the Coalition took power, the future Minister for Universities and Science, David Willetts, stated that:

> 'Our first principle is college autonomy. One of the things that always strikes me when I visit colleges is the long and proud history that so many of them have – for example, as local mechanics' institutes serving the needs of local employers. The Conservative in me is attracted by the idea of strong local institutions acting as glue in the local community... So I confirm that we will set you free.' (Willetts 2009)

After years of New Labour's 'policy hysteria' (Avis 2009), such promises may have held a certain appeal. But, whilst various organisations responsible for regulatory and developmental functions across the FE sector have either been abolished or radically cut back since 2010, the Coalition's notion of freedom is deeply rooted within a neo-liberal discourse of market competition and consumer choice; and, whilst New Labour actively encouraged private and voluntary providers to enter the FE marketplace, the current Government has driven privatisation much further than its predecessors. One example of this is the Employer Ownership of

Skills pilot. Run by PriceWaterhouseCoopers, this initiative offers employers direct access, in the first instance, to £250 million of public money 'to design and deliver their own training solutions' (UKCES 2012). So far, companies including Siemens, BAE Systems and Aria Foods UK have been significant beneficiaries of the scheme, which effectively subsidises the activities of private companies with public money (Sloman 2013, 10-11).

Apprenticeships are strongly linked to the privatisation of post-compulsory education and training and, whilst they are promoted as a response to skill shortages, they are also being used as a way of providing employers with ownership and control of the FE system and, perhaps more importantly, the funding. The Government's promotion of apprenticeships is also part of a discourse which seeks to valorise work-related learning as an alternative to academic study, at least for less privileged young people. The term 'apprenticeship' has long been associated with notions of craft, skill and job-security and there is no doubt it holds a certain appeal, especially to young working-class people and their parents. This, in turn, allows certain views about the value of 'hands-on' learning as a viable alternative to dry and abstract academic learning to be promoted, at least to certain sections of the population. Either way, there has been a great increase in the take-up of apprenticeships since the Coalition came to power, and it is important to note that some of these play a positive role in helping young people into employment. In other cases, however, employers have simply rebranded existing jobs as apprenticeships in order to access state funding. Moreover, in many instances, the training offered is very different from any traditional conception of an apprenticeship and certain programmes stretch the credulity of the term (Sloman 2013). Government nevertheless remains bullish:

'Apprenticeships are at the heart of our mission to rebuild the economy, giving young people the chance to learn a trade, build their careers, and create a truly world-class, highly-skilled workforce that can compete and thrive in the fierce global race we are in. There are record numbers of people taking up an apprenticeship, with a million starting one in the last few years.' (Cameron 2013)

Whatever the strengths or limitations of particular programmes, there is no doubt that apprenticeships and similar forms of vocational training have been shamelessly oversold by the Coalition as the solution to a range of problems. This is particularly the case with the enduring problem of youth unemployment, although this phenomenon is rooted at least as much in a chronic lack of demand for young people's labour as in any deficits in their skills, abilities, attitudes and dispositions. It is important to remember that the success of any education or training initiative will always be limited without concomitant intervention in labour and product markets, and the stimulation of the demand for employment (Sloman 2013). Fortunately, however, Ed Miliband's Real Jobs Guarantee for unemployed 18-24 year olds is one sign that key figures within the Labour Party are beginning to come to terms with this (Miliband 2012).

Alongside demands for a more 'hands-on' vocational curriculum, Coalition thinking stresses the need for different forms of learning to take place within different types of institution. This can be seen in the proposal to create up to 40 university technical colleges (UTCs) across England. Alongside qualifications in English, mathematics, science and IT, these institutions will offer technical education to 14-19 year olds in areas such as engineering; construction; sport and health sciences; land and environmental services; and hair and beauty. What is clear, however, is that vocational education clearly remains a second class option in comparison to academic education. This is evident in Prime Minister Cameron's views on UTCs which mix hyperbole with a discourse of deficit.

> 'The next great poverty-busting structural change we need – the expansion of University Technical Colleges – offering first-class technical skills to those turned off by purely academic study.' (Cameron, 2010).

Meanwhile, key Conservative thinkers within the Coalition seek to reassert 'traditional' academic values and to separate the academic from the vocational. Whilst New Labour rejected Tomlinson's (DfES 2004) proposal to formally break the academic-vocational divide through the creation of integrated diplomas, its period in power nevertheless resulted in some 'blurring' between vocational and academic learning. This occurred, for example, through the redefinition of General National Vocational Qualifications as 'applied' A-Levels and GCSEs, and through promoting the combination of academic and vocational study at 16+ following the reforms of 'Curriculum 2000', albeit with limited impact. In contrast, Coalition policy promotes more rigid divisions and increased exclusivity in academic education, for example, through allowing schools to 'filter out' pupils identified as less academic at an early stage and transfer these young people to FE colleges. This, alongside granting schools greater powers to suspend and expel students, is likely to increase the flow of less able students into FE and to reinforce vocational learning's subordinate status (Allen 2010).

Further education after the Coalition

Much will need to be done across all sectors of education after the Coalition loses power. Not least of these tasks should be a decluttering of the institutional landscape. The current jungle of organisations delivering education and training is both socially divisive and incredibly difficult for ordinary people to understand. Unequal possession of economic, social and cultural capital gives unequal access to different forms of education, and political decisions since the 1980s have ensured that those holding more of the various forms of capital have experienced continued advantage in gaining access to privileged forms of education (Ball 2003). Institutional competition and consumer choice benefit those most able to manipulate market forces and, whilst there is a strong case for reducing both institutional and curricular complexity throughout the education system, for post-compulsory education and training the best and most straightforward solution was first suggested well over 30 years ago: the creation of a national system of tertiary colleges.

The term tertiary college is sometimes used to describe any institution which provides a combination of academic and vocational programmes but, in their purest form, tertiary colleges are the sole providers of publicly-funded post-16 education in any given area, except that which is located in establishments of higher education (RCU 2003, 1). Under a truly tertiary system there are no school sixth forms, sixth-form colleges or other providers of education and training; young people of all abilities progress from local schools to a single organisation providing a broad, inclusive curriculum. Tertiary colleges also serve the needs of adult students and provide a wide range of education and training opportunities to the community more generally. Full-time and part-time courses, vocational, pre-vocational and academic education all take place within one institution: the traditionally divergent streams of academic and vocational education are united. In other words, tertiary colleges are effectively comprehensive institutions for post-school education and training.

England's first tertiary college was established in 1970 when Devon LEA abolished school sixth-forms in Exeter and created a single post-16 college in their place. Some other authorities followed suit and by the end of the decade 15 such institutions existed across England. Somewhat ironically given their hostility towards the principles of comprehensive education, Conservative-controlled LEAs, particularly those in rural areas with small, unviable sixth-forms and under-used FE colleges, were amongst the first to establish tertiary colleges. In contrast, tertiary re-organisation made less progress in Labour-controlled urban authorities. Many Labour councillors believed that allowing comprehensive schools to have their own sixth-forms would provide an equitable system in place of grammar schools. Some schoolteachers argued there would be a drop in standards in schools without sixth-forms. Often parents worried about the 'freedoms' offered by the more mature environment found outside schools (Allen and Ainley 2007, 53).

From the early 1970s onwards, a combination of factors brought increasing pressure on the education system. The economic crisis which followed the OPEC oil boycott of 1973 and the ensuing collapse of much of the UK's traditional industrial base brought significant consequences (Ainley 2007, 369), as did the problem of falling school rolls. A particular problem for FE was the curtailment of the supply of day-release students which had traditionally provided the majority of its learners. Consequently many colleges diversified their offer and participation in further education, especially on a full-time basis, grew steadily throughout the 1970s as FE colleges began to embrace new types of students. Gradually, colleges shifted away from their technical roots and became more inclusive organisations offering a broad range of vocational, pre-vocational and academic courses (Lucas 1999, 18). Another important development was the creation of the Manpower Services Commission and the introduction of various training and re-training schemes for the growing ranks of the unemployed, which also brought new constituencies of adults and young people into colleges (Ainley and Corney 1990).

As is the case today, during the 1970s successive governments were focused on reducing public expenditure. For local authorities the re-organisation of post-compulsory education was a frequent response to the pressure to cut costs, and some decided simply to concentrate sixth-form provision in certain schools, leaving others to concentrate on 11-16 year-olds. Elsewhere, LEAs encouraged neighbouring schools to share staff, students and facilities by forming sixth-form consortia. Most of these arrangements were, however, fraught with logistical problems and usually unsuccessful (Terry 1987, 10-11). Other authorities chose to close school sixth forms and create separate sixth-form colleges for students continuing with academic studies after reaching the minimum school leaving age. This model offered some advantages over some other forms of post-16 re-organisation – including greater clarity of structure and the ability of sixth-form colleges to offer a broader range of courses than school sixth forms (Terry 1987, 9). However, despite their name, sixth-form colleges were established under Schools Regulations and were usually set up on former grammar school premises. Sixth-form colleges remain distinctive in both their predominantly academic goals and the relative social advantage of their intake; in many ways, their culture remains similar to that of schools (Foster 2005, 21). The creation of sixth-form colleges may have appeased middle-class interests, but left a number of problems unresolved. One issue was the often considerable overlap between sixth-form colleges and neighbouring FE colleges. Normally FE colleges would take the largest number of post-school students in a given area but, like sixth-form colleges, would sometimes also have significant numbers of A-level students. Nevertheless, most FE colleges continued to have a predominantly vocational curriculum and, therefore, continued to suffer from an image of being second-best. Faced with such a scenario, some LEAs adopted a radical option – 'going tertiary'.

In 1979, the incoming Conservative Government set up a post-16 working party under the chairmanship of Under-Secretary of State for Education, Neil Macfarlane. The group's remit included a survey of work carried out by local authorities in rationalising post-16 education; an assessment of future demand for various types of education and training; an examination of the relationship between schools and FE colleges; and a consideration of the cost-effectiveness of existing provision. The Macfarlane Committee found a range of evidence in favour of tertiary re-organisation, including cost savings through the rationalisation of existing provision; the ability of tertiary colleges to offer a wider programme of full-time and part-time courses than is possible through other arrangements; and the opportunity for young people to select the courses best suited to their needs (Macfarlane 1980, 31). Consequently, Macfarlane initially recommended that, for both educational and cost reasons, a national system of tertiary colleges should be created. This was a truly radical proposal with potentially far-reaching consequences and, if implemented, would have meant the dissolution of school-sixth forms and sixth-form colleges across England. The 'Cinderella service' would, for the first time, have been brought into the mainstream and the ethos of comprehensive education would have been extended to the post-compulsory level.

Unsurprisingly, senior figures in the Conservative Party were alarmed at Macfarlane's proposals and, following Lady Young's intervention on the behalf of Prime Minister, Margaret Thatcher, Macfarlane was forced to climb down (David 1981, 764). Consequently, the final draft of the Macfarlane Report recommended only that LEAs consider tertiary re-organisation in light of their own local circumstances. A national tertiary policy was thought impracticable because of 'the realities of existing investment', 'local preferences' and the claimed 'success of many "all through" schools' (Macfarlane 1980, 36).

Effectively Macfarlane fudged the issue of tertiary re-organisation. Nevertheless, some local authorities pressed on and by the early-1990s almost 70 tertiary colleges had been established, although often school sixth-forms and sixth-form colleges were allowed to exist alongside so-called tertiary colleges. The lack of a national policy also meant that, even in the few areas where a fully tertiary model was implemented, competition for students with institutions in neighbouring authorities undermined the tertiary principle. The 1988 Education Reform Act made tertiary re-organisation considerably more difficult by creating Grant Maintained (GM) status. This allowed some schools to opt out of LEA control and enabled GM schools to set-up sixth-forms outside the local authority framework. The threat of leaving LEA control was also used by some schools as a defence against the prospect of re-organisation. The possibility of creating more tertiary colleges was effectively extinguished when local authorities lost all responsibility for running further education following the 1992 Further and Higher Education Act.

Had Macfarlane's initial recommendation – the creation of a national system of tertiary colleges – been implemented, this would have helped to create a more coherent institutional framework than had existed hitherto – and a far more transparent system of post-compulsory education than exists today. Rather than competition and duplication of provision, national tertiary reorganisation could have been used to encourage institutional co-operation and innovative practice. Across the country, students would have been given access to a wider range of courses and greater flexibility of study in both the number and type of subjects available to them. Whilst we need to remember that education cannot compensate for all society's ills (Bernstein 2000, 59), the way in which education is structured and delivered can exacerbate or ameliorate inequality. The creation of a national system of tertiary colleges would go at least some way towards reducing the deep inequalities that characterise the English education system today.

Research suggests that tertiary colleges offer significant educational advantages in comparison to other forms of post-compulsory education and training, and that these benefits are experienced by students from across a broad spectrum of ability and background. Drawing comparisons between tertiary, general FE and sixth-form colleges, a study conducted by the Responsive Colleges Unit (RCU 2003) found tertiary colleges to have higher achievement rates at almost all levels and much better success in encouraging learners to progress on to higher levels of study. It also found they have significantly better retention rates than general FE colleges, with levels almost as high as those found in sixth-form colleges, despite having a far more diverse curriculum and a much more inclusive ethos; and that a genuinely tertiary structure helps to increase overall participation rates, especially for students from relatively deprived backgrounds. Moreover, tertiary colleges enable students to access a wider range of courses and have greater flexibility of choice in the options available to them – and, importantly, this includes access to a range of specialist and 'minority' subjects normally reserved for the privileged. With full-time and part-time students; arts, sciences and technology; general and vocational courses offered within one institution, the potential to begin to break down – or at least reduce – the barriers between academic education and applied training becomes possible (Cotterell and Heley 1981, 10-11).

Perhaps the Macfarlane Report represents a key moment that has been lost forever. The economic and political climate since the time of the Report has run contrary to the principles of the tertiary college movement, and there is no doubt that the Coalition is fiercely hostile to the ideals of comprehensive education. Yet, despite all this, tertiary reorganisation may still return to the agenda. A new government committed to increasing social justice would obviously be needed to revive the tertiary college movement but other, more expedient factors, also mean that, in many ways, tertiary colleges are the obvious answer to a number of immediate and pressing questions. For example, for the foreseeable future at least, it will be necessary for governments to operate within strict spending constraints – and, as we have seen, the tertiary college allows education and training to be delivered in a more cost-effective way than is possible through other arrangements. Other developments, such as raising the compulsory age of participation to 18, present both educational and logistical challenges to which only tertiary colleges can provide a satisfactory solution: a broad, flexible curriculum and an inclusive ethos is necessary to engage disadvantaged and marginalised young people who would not otherwise be participating in education and training.

Much will need to be done across all sectors of education once the

Coalition is gone and, whilst the logistical and political challenges involved in creating a national system of tertiary colleges should not be underestimated, it is in many ways the obvious answer for post-school education and training. Having said this, young people still need to be provided with meaningful labour market opportunities however robust or well-delivered their education. Labour market intervention to stimulate the demand for work and for particular forms of knowledge and skill is necessary to provide young people with meaningful employment opportunities and the motivation to study. This will mean a radically different approach not only to organising and providing education and training but to social and economic policy more broadly.

References
Ainley, P. (2007) 'Across the great divide. From a welfare state to a new market state: the case of VET', *Journal of Vocational Education and Training*, 59 (3) 369-384.

Ainley, P. & Bailey, B. (1997) *The Business of Learning: staff and student experiences of further education in the 1990s*. London: Cassell.

Ainley, P. & Corney, M. (1990) *Training for the Future: the rise and fall of the Manpower Services Commission*. London: Cassell.

Allen, M. (2010) *Education's 'Credibility Crunch': the upper secondary years* http://radicaled.wordpress.com/ (accessed 21 November 2010).

Allen, M. & Ainley, P. (2007) *Education make you fick, innit? What's gone wrong in England's schools, colleges and universities and how to start putting it right.* London: Tufnell.

Avis, J. (2009) 'Further education: policy hysteria, competitiveness and performativity', *British Journal of Sociology of Education*, 30 (5) 653-662.

Avis, J. (2011) 'More of the same? New Labour, the Coalition and education: markets, localism and social justice', *Educational Review,* 63 (4) 421-438.

Bailey, B. (1987) 'The development of technical education', *History of Education*, 16 (1) 49-65.

Bailey, B. (2002) 'Further education', in *A century of education,* ed. R. Aldrich. London: RoutledgeFalmer, . 54-74.

Ball, S.J. (2003) *Class Strategies and the Education Market: the Middle Classes and Social Advantage.* London: RoutledgeFalmer.

Bernstein, B. (2000) *Pedagogy, symbolic control and identity: theory, research, critique* (revised edition) Oxford: Rowman and Littlefield.

Burchill, F. (1998) *Five Years of Change: A Survey of Pay, Terms and Conditions in the Further Education Sector Five Years after Incorporation.* London: NATFHE.

Cabinet Office (2008) *Realising Britain's Potential: Future Strategic Challenges for Britain. London: Cabinet Office Strategy Strategic Challenges for Britain.* London: Cabinet Office.

Callaghan, J. (1976) Ruskin College Speech, *Times Educational*

Supplement 22 October.

Cameron, D. (2010) http://www.utcolleges.org/ (accessed 24th January 2011)

Cameron, D. (2013) http://www.number10.gov.uk/news/david-cameron-apprenticeships-central-torebuilding-the-economy/ (accessed 23rd July 2013)

Coffield, F. (2006) *Running ever faster down the wrong road,* Inaugural Lecture. London: London University Institute of Education. December 5[th.]

Cotterell, A. & Heley, E. (1981) *Tertiary: A Radical Approach to Post-Compulsory Education.* Cheltenham: Stanley Thornes.

David, N., Baroness of Romsey (1981) Education: expenditure cuts. House of Lords debate. *Hansard* (418) 761-850. London: HMSO.

Department of Business Innovation and Skills (2012) *Professionalism in further education. Interim report of the Independent Review Panel.* London: DBIS.

Department for Education and Skills (2004) *14-19 Curriculum and Qualifications Reform: final report of the working group on 14-19 reform.* Annesley: DfES.

Fisher, R. & Simmons, R. (2012) 'Liberal Conservatism, Vocationalism and Further Education in England', *Globalisation, Societies and Education,* 10 (1) 31-51.

Foster, A. (2005) *Realising the Potential: a review of the role of further education colleges*. London: DfES Publications.

Further Education Funding Council (1998) Towards an inclusive learning society in the new millennium – the contribution of further education, in Education and Employment Committee, Appendix 4. Coventry: FEFC.

Further Education Unit (1979) A Basis for Choice. London: FEU.

Gove, M. (2010) Speech to the National College Annual Conference, Birmingham, 16th June. Available at http://www.education.gov.uk/inthenews/speeches/a0061371/micha el-gove-to-the-national-college-annual-conference-birmingham (accessed 9th September 2012).

Gravatt, J. & Silver, R. (2000) 'Partnerships with the community', in A. Smithers and P. Robinson (eds) *Further Education Reformed*. London: Falmer.

Hodgson, A. & Spours, K. (2006) 'An analytical framework for policy engagement: the contested case of 14-19 reform in England'. *Journal of Education Policy,* 21(6) 679-696.

Miliband, E. (2012) http:// www.labour.org.uk/ed-milibands-speech-to-labours-youth-conference (accessed 23 July 2013).

Lucas, N. (2004) *Teaching in Further Education: New Perspectives for a Changing Context*. London: Bedford Way Papers.

Macfarlane, N. (1980) *Education for 16-19 year-olds: a review undertaken for the government and the local authority associations*. Stanmore: DES.

Orr, K. & Simmons, R. (2010) 'Dual identities: the in-service teacher trainee experience in the English further education sector', *Journal of Vocational Education and Training*, 62 (1) 75-88.

Randle, K. & Brady, N. (1997) 'Managerialism and professionalism in the Cinderella sector', *Journal of Vocational Education and Training*, 49 (1) 121-139.

Responsive College Unit (2003) *Research into the comparative performance of tertiary colleges*. Preston: RCU.

Richardson, W. (2007) 'In search of the further education of young people in post-war England', *Journal of Vocational Education and Training,* 59 (3) 385-418.

Simmons, R. (2008) 'Golden Years? Further education colleges under local authority control', *Journal of Further and Higher Education*, 32 (4) 359-371.

Simmons, R. (2009) 'Further education in England and the lost opportunity of the Macfarlane Report', *Journal of Further and Higher Education,* 33 (2) 159-169.

Simmons, R. (2010) 'Globalisation, neo-liberalism and vocational learning: the case of English further education colleges', *Research in Post-Compulsory Education*, 15 (4) 363-376.

Sloman, M. (2013) 'Training for skills in crisis – a critique and recommendations', *Training Journal* LandD 2020 project paper.

Terry, D. (1987) *The Tertiary College: Assuring Our Future*. Milton Keynes: Open University Press.

UKCES (2012) http://www.ukces.org.uk/assets/ukces/docs/employer-ownership/employer-ownership-of-skills-prospectus-final-version.pdf (accessed 23 July 2013).

Waitt, I. (ed) (1980) *College Administration*. London: NATFHE.

Willetts, D. (2009) Speech at the Association of Colleges conference http://www.davidwilletts.co.uk/2009/11/19/speech-at-the-association-of-colleges-conference/ (accessed 14 September 2010).

Chapter 6

Too Great Expectations of Higher Education

Patrick Ainley

Introduction

Nowhere has the Thatcherite mantra of raising standards through competition unraveled faster than in higher education. As all teachers know, 'standards' are not merely a code for valuing traditional academic knowledge and assessment over any other approach. They are also a means of measurement so as to stick numbers on qualities that are otherwise unquantifiable and rank them in order of consumer choice. This process in education, as in health (see Leys & Player 2011), was completed under the New Labour government's marketization of public services. As a result, 'delivery agents' – as schools, colleges and universities with their staffs – have become, are in competition with each other for 'consumers' – as parents, pupils and students have become. In the name of raising standards, rival claims to 'excellence' and 'quality' are monitored and inspected by central government agencies like Ofsted, which relentlessly set 'agents' new targets to fail. However ruthless and desperate the struggle for survival in education becomes, this is still what was has been called a 'quasi-market' as no money is directly involved. Save in the private schools, consumers do not pay more for higher standards and private providers seeking profit for investors from the services they offer are limited, though repeatedly encouraged. Competition between public sector providers is therefore for 'customers' to whom monetary value is attached by the central state, enabling some institutions to accrue surpluses whilst others are increasingly indebted. Mergers and closures, conglomerations and chains thus follow in a market-led restructuring of education such as has already occurred and continues in FE.

Higher education is an important exception to this moneyless marketization as fees for English undergraduate home students were introduced for the first time in 1997 when grants were also abolished, leaving students without other income dependent on maintenance loans on top of repaying their fees. Paradoxically however, a market still does not exist with variable prices for different 'standards' of provision. This is because nearly all 'providers'/ universities have raised their fees to the maximum £9,000 currently allowed and outside provision is still limited. When fees are uncapped, it can be anticipated that 'top universities' will raise their prices to whatever the market will bear and institutions will be strung out along a range of variably and individually priced courses so that a free market will then exist, as it already does in postgraduate provision.

Meanwhile, because student loans for fees do not have to be repaid for so long and only then if earning above the median wage, 'customers'/ students are still applying – although some whole groups have been lost (adults and part-timers long ago, many white working-class males more recently). (This could change if repayment terms are altered by government to encourage private speculators to buy the student loan book and/or if repayments were to begin at a lower threshold, say £18k instead of £21k. The government will have to do something since it has already acknowledged it does not expect more than a third of what will be a £191 billion debt to be recovered by 2046 when outstanding balances will begin to be written off after 30 years (McGettigan

2013). (No wonder HE Minister, David Willetts, is under pressure to leave! He, however, calculates on reducing student numbers drastically.) Also, because the 2.1 degree that is now obtained by half of graduates has become the new threshold for perhaps half of all jobs available to young people, it is worth becoming endebted up to £27k student loan + maintenance loan + 3% interest on top of rate of inflation on both (McGettigan estimated an average of £40k) in hopes of the '15 per cent higher lifetime earnings than people with lower qualifications' that the Million+ group of former-polytechnic universities claim as their 'graduate premium' (Hadfield *et al* 2012). Or instead, entering oversubscribed 'apprenticeships' – 'professional' or not – as long as they lead to a job; 'internships' and post-graduate courses similarly. As Martin Allen points out, 'Pupils and students will do anything they have to to get the grades they need'.

This is where the mantra of 'standards' falls down, as students pay more for less, so that many courses offer notoriously little in the way of knowledge or learning and relations between teachers and students are corrupted as all involved pretend that they do. 20% of UK students 'read' (!) Business Studies but many more take business-related modules on other courses reduced towards bite-sized learning in a repetitive carousel of non-cumulative learning guided only by 'student choice' (McArdle-Clinton 2008). Lecturers are also locked into a *simulacrum* of supposedly 'vocationally-related' training that has less and less to do with students' real lives and experiences. Even – or especially – at the 'highest' academic levels, exam regurgitation tests levels of literacy as a proxy for more or less expensively acquired cultural capital. Further down the food-chain, young people lacking other opportunities seek *The Pleasures of Being a Student* (Cheeseman 2011) on an increasingly pre-packaged experience without much thought to what they will do afterwards when many inevitably return to their parental homes. Especially young women, who are generally better qualified for entry and have been the majority in most subjects – including prestigious ones like medicine and law – in HE worldwide for some time (details in Leathwood and Reid 2009). For those nominally 'full-time' students who live at home to save money, attending local HE is often peripheral to their social lives and supposedly 'part-time' work. Yet still parents and teachers, schools and colleges urge students on to what many of them see as a *Triumph of Emptiness* (Alvesson 2013).

So what went wrong?

All this has been achieved by placing *Students at the heart of the system* as the 2011 White Paper is titled. Even without subsequent legislation (see McGettigan *o.c.*), this marked the end, not only of higher education as it has developed since the war but – more broadly – of the whole effort to reform society through education (Apple 2013). It closed a phase of progressive reform that began in 1963 with the recommendation by Robbins of the expansion of HE beyond the limited pool who were previously considered educable to all 'qualified by ability and attainment' to benefit. Robbins thus preserved a selective system and was not an entitlement or even expectation for all who graduated high school as in the republican French and original US model. Following Robbins, the official introduction of comprehensive schools from 1965 was not accompanied by curricular reform so that comprehensives were left competing for still selective university entry with the surviving grammars and private schools on the uneven playing field of academic A-levels, even after the introduction of GCSEs in 1986. Primary schools were, however, freed for child-centred education while there was also further growth of FE and technical education. Unlike 11+ selection, which became a thing of the past in 80 % of

English secondary schools and more in Scotland and Wales, reforming state education at all levels no longer aimed to reinforce existing social hierarchies but to break down class divisions by opening equal opportunities to careers for all. The logic of comprehensive reform carried forward to inclusion of children with special needs, a common exam at 16 and a National Curriculum presented to teachers as an entitlement for all, as well as – more recently – widening participation in HE to nearly half of 18-30 year olds.

Now Coalition education policy aims at a *Great Reversal* (Allen and Ainley 2013) to minority HE. A cap-free market in fees variable by course and institution could leave Arts and Humanities to overseas students and others who are seriously rich at elite and surviving campus universities. Other universities and colleges could collapse around their technical departments for as long as Science, Technology, Engineering and Medicine STEM subjects remain centrally funded, the rest merging into local e-learning hubs proffering two-year degrees by part-time and distance provision if they are not bought-out or taken-over (see McGettigan again). For some time a tertiary tripartism has distinguished internationally selecting and researching Russells from nationally recruiting and mainly teaching campus universities as against locally clearing and training institutions (Weyers and Ainley 2008).

This did not all happen just because post-modernist academics lost the plot! The 'literary turn' that took over the humanities and social sciences in the 1980s created a new academic orthodoxy misapprehending wider changes in Western society. Rather than the result of some new Foucauldian discourse, they were a consequence of economic and technical shifts in employment triggered by change in the organic composition of capital exacerbating the falling rate of profit and leading in turn to speculative instead of productive investment. They were imposed by political changes leading to a new form of global, 'free-market' state in place of the national Keynesian welfare state in which progressive and social democratic change had been possible. Despite Bernstein's 1970 warning that *Education cannot compensate for society*, teachers at all levels typically continued to believe that it could. This was partly because of our own experience of education, particularly higher education which grew from c.2%, mostly young men, in 1945 to c.7%, including a growing proportion of women, by the time the baby-boomers went to university in the late 1960s. This was a generation of students most of whose parents – even if middle class – did not themselves go to higher education but these students' HE experience made them middle class if they were not already.

The new universities of the 1960s aimed to spread (more thinly, their detractors said) traditional HE in the arts, humanities and social sciences, while extending sciences to the Colleges of Advanced Technology elevated to University status. Instead of more Robbins universities, the polytechnics from 1965-1992 aimed at both an HE on the cheap and a new HE for adult students living locally (as in Robinson 1968). Despite some brave experiments, eg. Independent Study at East London Polytechnic and Lancaster University, this proved illusory (see Robbins 1988). So too did the latest phase of widening participation to HE sustained on a reduced unit of resource from 2003-2011 by faith in the transformative powers of new ICT to include nearly half of 18-30 women at least – fallen by 2012 to c. one third of 18+ women and a quarter of men. Recruitment overall was down about 10% in 2012 but has recovered somewhat this year, though academic confidence that 'normal service has resumed' cannot be taken for granted. Nearly all universities raised their entry thresholds last year; now many have brought them down again. All but Oxbridge plus LSE were forced into clearing this year for at least some subjects, leaving others in the expanded 'top' Russell Group to compete with each other to attract AAB (last year) and ABB (this year) A-level grade students. Some, eg. Southampton and Liverpool, lost out badly in 2012 as Bristol broke the cartel to take in extra numbers. The 'Real Russells', by contrast, characteristically restrict their undergraduate intake to increase demand and leave their academics more room for research. This year the competition is even more ferocious.

'Widening participation' has not led to fair or equal access to equal types of higher education or outcomes in the labour market. Nor has it increased social mobility to 'transform lives' as academics sometimes fancy that they do. (UCU recently conducted a campaign to boost this self-image among its members). In fact, the opposite is the case; as elsewhere in education, the system functions to keep people in their place. Social divisions are heightening and hardening in HE, where the general rule is that the older the university, the younger, whiter, more male and posher its students. (Warwick University is an exception that only proves this rule.) More Black and minority ethnic applicants may enter HE but they graduate with lower grades at lower status HEIs. As David summarized, there are *'systemic and systematic forms of inequality for individuals and institutions across subjects and levels of education'* (2009, 150 Italicized for emphasis in original). Like Thatcher's previous encouragement of home ownership, or at least mortgage borrowing, that contributed to the subsequent bubble in unproductive capital, this presented itself as a professionalization of the proletariat while disguising a proletarianisation of the professions, as automation leading to the deskilling and outsourcing that were evident to Braverman amongst US craft workers in 1974 have worked their way up the employment hierarchy to previously secure professionals. This includes notably an academic profession reduced towards the contractual conditions of wage labour.

Teachers are another case in point, professionalizing themselves by association with HE Schools of Education from FE trade training colleges (a move now being reversed by Gove back to an apprentice training model in schools). But with 'standards' dictated by central government agency, teacher training is also an example of increasingly prevalent FE in HE as education is reduced to competence training. (This is not to disparage FE – indeed, FE and HE would ideally combine in what Silver 2004 called 'Thick HE', going 'further' at the same time as going 'higher'. Nor does it fail to recognize that you cannot have education without training but you can – and increasingly do – have training without education.) Nevertheless, teacher training's association with HE has to be defended and extended beyond standards-based training towards a research-informed teacher education. This would be opposed to Gove's private school model in which teachers are born and not made, so no training – let alone education – is necessary (see Simon 1985). Possibly, such training of 'the schools workforce' as the New Labour government began calling it, exemplifies the new correspondence with employment – if there is one and education is not economically dysfunctional save as a means of social control – because many HE students now aspire to graduate to similar service sector professional and paraprofessional roles as are available in schools to teachers and their assistants.

As for research – which Weaver (1974) indicated is often mistaken to be privileged as 'knowledge production' over teaching as 'knowledge reproduction' within HE, as well as over schools and colleges – as Harvey noted as long ago as 1986 in *The Condition of*

Postmodernity (160),

> 'the universities in the industrially developed countries are shifting from being guardians of national knowledge to ancillaries in the production of knowledge for global corporations'.

Marketised by successive competitive research assessment/ excellence exercises,

> 'Research selectivity has been used not just to concentrate research funding but to restructure the system by determining institutional missions and status.' (Brown and Carasso 2013, 134)

Meanwhile, in the new mixed economy, private sector penetration of increasingly entrepreneurial public universities is perverting the 1918 Haldane principle that public funds for research should be allocated on the basis of academic criteria, not political or economic considerations. This is producing new medico-industrial university complexes far removed from Polanyian ideals of 'communities of science'. Most science students, however, graduate to be lab-technicians if they are lucky while many engineering departments in F&HE have closed for lack of employment for their students. Traditional empiricism still inhibits cross-disciplinarity and public intellectuality, so that science and higher education generally has reneged on its role of critically learning from the past in order not to repeat it in the future – particularly in relation to climate change (see Ainley 2008).

Rather than responding to the needs of a non-existent 'knowledge economy' in which supposedly high skilled jobs predominate over the mass of deskilled and routinized employment that actually exists in a society in which the occupational class structure has gone pear-shaped, education is increasingly unable to fulfil the expectations it raises. It is thus losing its validity as a way forward for the younger generations. Unconnected to possibilities for practice, displaying knowledge for assessment has replaced learning. This *simulacrum* of study disguises the decline in attainment – if not the increase in effort – all teachers recognize. Developing an alternative requires a different set of values and concepts to address the perennial question of what education should be for. Nevertheless, any alternative for young people – as for society as a whole – must begin with the economy and an end to austerity in the UK and EU (see Patomaki 2013). Recovery also has to be sustainable. To think that things can go on as they are adds only to what Alvesson (2013, *o.c* 216-7) calls the 'functional stupidity' to which he sees education, mass entertainment, the media and especially advertising, contributing – 'a socially supported lack of reflexivity, substantive reasoning, and justification [that]… means you refrain from critical thinking, reflection and the posing of broader questions about values, ideals, and representations of reality.'

So what are the alternatives?

The market is so omnivorous even positive alternatives, like efforts at Lincoln University to do away with grading, tend to get assimilated as brands if they are successful. System-wide reform is therefore necessary (see Burns 2012) as well as larger social change, such as return to progressive taxation rather than any proposed graduate tax in place of fees, even reduced ones (to £6,000 as Labour proposed – though whether this is still their policy or whether they would ever implement it in government is not clear). Peter Scott at Brighton University's 2013 Convention for Higher Education was surely right to call for 'a revival of radical thinking about HE', whilst 'accepting that HE needed reform but not this reform'. (Cf. Camila Vallejo, the Chilean student leader, widely quoted on the internet as saying, 'We want to improve the educational system but not this one. We must move towards a more inclusive, truly democratic and just system.') Therefore to celebrate and not apologise for a mass system and fight for an increase in student numbers not 'consolidation' – 'the job is only half done!' as Scott said. This is not to demand everyone necessarily attends HE at 18. Many do not want to – including many who are there! There should however be a universal entitlement to do so based on a general certificate of high school graduation. This will require what Spours and Hodgson (2012) call *A unified ecosystem vision* of schools and colleges in relation to universities.

In such a regionally integrated learning system, for students for whom, as Gerald Graff remarks, 'the very words "education" and "academic" are opaque' (2003, 274), the whole purpose of university has to be represented. Many students do not see the point of discussion from different perspectives, nor do they understand how to distinguish between them with reference to evidence or argument. They have not heard Clint Eastwood in the film *Every which way but loose* dismiss opinions as resembling a piece of anatomy common to men and women: 'Everyone's got one!' Many students lack the confidence to make warranted assertions and fall back upon clichés or their own personal 'feelings' and prejudices. Thus, like our former-Prime Minister Blair they only know what they believe, instead of, like the philosopher of science, Michael Polanyi (1956, 266), believing in what they know.

In Scots and US universities there is a first-year foundation that is impossible in England – necessary and desirable though this is to bring students up to speed – because it would represent an extra year's fee. In the USA, this year makes space for courses that attempt some intellectual socialization into the on-going conversations of academic culture, unlike our own inductions which largely restrict themselves to study skills, time-management and tours of the library and IT facilities, including the student support that has become virtually virtual. The crisis of student (academic) literacy which such foundation years might help to address is combined with one of legitimacy as the widened student body desperately hopes their expensively purchased degrees will gain them what Ken Roberts (personal communication) calls 'an "intermediate" starting occupation' on graduation. This at least forced some academics to agree what is important in the subjects they taught as they sought to adapt tertiary level learning to new generations of students in the way comprehensive school teachers previously struggled to open secondary schooling to the mass of the population. That this effort was first made in 'The Bad Universities' – as defined negatively by *The Times* 'Good University Guide' – contributes to the denigration of such efforts, seen by the elite as abandoning 'academic standards'.

Moreover, it is in these 'Bad Universities' that the pressure is on to reduce traditional programmes towards two-year degrees, either as Foundation 'degrees' or as three-year courses delivered over two years to include the summer in order to utilise plant and staff more efficiently. Or merely as preliminary to post-graduate – perhaps doctoral – 'real HE' since so many taught Masters now churn around in one year. (Instead of reducing course lengths, a 2+2+2+2 model of Part 1 and 2 four-year undergraduate degree, followed by two years Masters and two years Doctorate would be much simpler and preferable to the confusion that currently exists; it would also accord with the original 1988 Bologna declaration on credit accumulation and transfer across the European region.)

'The Bad Universities' are also those where most students live locally and are in part-time if not full-time employment – sometimes in several part-time jobs simultaneously if they can find them (see O'Leary 2013). Their students also have the greatest needs and disabilities such as dyslexia (over-diagnosed though this probably is). Raised and differentiated fees will heighten instead of concealing these differences, pitting students and staff in competition with one another; a competition in which it is tempting for Students Unions to join by pressing the claims of their members as consumers. Moreover, as Cheeseman remarks (2013), 'Student culture has reoriented itself over the years, away from institutionally specific local cultures to a national and increasingly international, mediated youth culture.' Pedagogic coherence can be recovered through emphasising the contributions to knowledge that students can make in their chosen academic disciplines or fields of practice through independent research, scholarship, creation or application in their final year. This should be made clear to undergraduates at induction and the first and second years of their programmes should build towards it.

Students can be progressively introduced to the debates integral to the on-going constitution of their field of study or application preparatory to making a contribution to it. They will thus become familiar with the canon of texts and experiments, or cases as exemplars, presenting the conceptual tools with which to order the field's information base. They can then recognise that the truth claims they make in the wider world of public debate and professional practice accord with the accepted criteria of scientific and logical proof and so go beyond personal admissions of opinion, belief or prejudice. *Expertise* (Collins & Evans 2007), combining skill and knowledge, can also be developed in final year dissertations to make creation, experiment, research or scholarship an integral part of the Independent Study of all students, rather than separating teaching from research. This in essence is the answer to the vexed question of research in HE: research must be generalised to as many teachers and students as possible, including in schools and colleges/ adult continuing education.

Generalising research/ scholarship/ experiment and creation does not preclude dedicated and state-funded specialist research institutes such as already exist in this and other countries, especially for 'Big Science', but in general teaching should be combined with research as a means of introducing students to an academic community that critically learns from the past to change behaviour in the future. The undergraduate dissertation can then be developed to emphasize the contribution that students can make to that continuing cultural conversation as the final degree demonstration of higher level graduateness. Such development will widen the still available critical space afforded by higher education in which a defence of the public university can be conducted (Holmwood 2012). This should bring together staff and students, instead of antagonising them in the way that putting customers/ *students at the heart of the system* does. Nor can (higher) education be merely for its own sake as Collini (2012) suggested. It is much more important than that!

As UNESCO's 1997 *Resolution on Higher Education* states: 'higher education is directed to human development and to the progress of society'. In a democratic society, deciding on the nature of development and progress (increasingly to recognize what is necessary for human survival and how to ensure it), is the common practice of citizens for which a general education in schools should not only prepare them for assumption of full and independent citizenship at 18 but engage them in from the earliest years. Such a foundational education should also be informed by the discussion,

119

research and scholarship preserved and developed by post-compulsory further, higher and adult continuing education in a process of critical cultural transmission, creation and recreation. This would transform learning at all levels to be no longer so obsessively dedicated to selection for employment. Students should learn about work as well as to work – a principle that should apply to all work experience and placements in schools as well as in colleges/ universities, including properly paid and regulated apprenticeships and internships.

The changing occupational structure, with so many employed part-time in a new social formation of a working-middle/ middle-working class in a class structure going pear-shaped, potentiates a base for support of such a progressive education. But, as ever, the insecurities of this precarious majority have been repeatedly directed by government and dominant media towards antagonism against the 'new rough' so-called 'underclass', presented as 'undeserving poor' and blamed for their own situation. The new class formation puts in question Grasmscian hegemony based upon a traditional working class but (at least according to Mason 2012) creates the possibility of resistance *Kicking Off Everywhere*, stimulated by new media. Certainly, the new generations have little chance to organise at their work, which is part-time and irregular at best, and the traditional political activities of their parents – like public meetings, let alone leafleting and lobbying – are felt to be ineffective and largely irrelevant, or at least too long-term, such is the urgency of youth's situation. However, in contrast to Standing 2011, who sees an almost inevitable conflict between the established and 'privileged' old working class and a new and youthful *precariat*, Allen and Ainley (*o.c.*) argue that a new politics will still need the old alliances. It therefore falls to labour movement organizations – not least because of their considerable resources and their continued ability to dislocate production – to move beyond simply defending their members' immediate interests. They need to develop policies recognizing that the majority of society are undermined by the latest degeneration of a moribund capitalism that is wasting its human as well as its natural resources. Higher education and its important constituency of increasingly disillusioned students remains a critical space in which to generate such alternatives.

References

Ainley, P. (2008) 'Education and Climate Change – some systemic connections' in *British Journal of Sociology of Education*, 29 (2) 213-223.

Allen, M. & Ainley, P. (2013) *The Great Reversal, Young People, Education and Employment in a Declining Economy* from www.radicaled.wordpress.com.

Alvesson, M. (2013) *The Triumph of Emptiness, Consumption, Higher Education and Work Organization*. Oxford: Oxford University Press.

Apple, M. (2013) *Can Education Change Society?* London: Routledge.

Bernstein, B. (1970) 'Education Cannot Compensate for Society' *New Society*, 26 Feb 1970, 344-7.

Braverman, H. (1974) *Labor and Monopoly Capital, The Degredation of Work in the Twentieth Century*. New York: Monthly Review Press.

Brown, R. & Carasso, H. (2013) *Everything for Sale? The marketization of UK higher education*. London: Routledge and the Society for Research into Higher Education.

Burns, L. (2012) 'The idea of a tertiary education system' in L. Coiffait (ed) *Blue Skies, New thinking about the future of higher education*. London: Pearson.

Cheeseman, M. (2013) 'Student Culture' in *Society for Research into Higher Education News*, July 2013, 18.

Cheeseman, M. (2011) *The Pleasures of Being a Student at the University of Sheffield*. Sheffield University unpublished PhD thesis.

Collini, S. (2012) *What Are Universities For?* Harmondsworth: Penguin.

Collins, H. & Evans, R. (2007) *Rethinking Expertise*. Chicago: University of Chicago Press.

David, M. (ed) (2009) *Improving learning by widening participation in higher education*. London: Routledge.

Department for Business, Innovation and Skills (2011) *Higher education: students at the heart of the system*, London: DBIS.

Graff, G. (2003) *Clueless in Academe, How schooling obscures the life of the mind*. New Haven: Yale UP.

Hadfield, M., Dhillon, J., Joplin, M. & Goffe, R. (2012) *Teaching that matters, Modern Universities Changing Lives.* Wolverhampton: University of Wolverhampton.

Harvey, D. (1986) *The Condition of Postmodernity, an Inquiry into the Origins of Cultural Change.* Oxford: Blackwell.

Holmwood, J. (ed) (2011) *A Manifesto for the Public University*, London : Bloomsbury.

HMSO (1963) *Higher Education.* London: HMSO. (The Robbins Report)

Leathwood, C. & Read, B. (2009) *Gender and the Changing Face of Higher Education, a Feminized Future?* Maidenhead: Open University Press and the Society for Research into Higher Education.

Leys, C. and Player, S. (2011) *The Plot Against the NHS.* London: Merlin.

Mason, P. (2012) *Why It's Kicking Off Everywhere.* London: Verso.

McArdle-Clinton, D. (2008) *The Consumer Experience of Higher Education, The Rise of Capsule Education.* London: Continuum.

McGettigan, A. (2013) *The Great University Gamble, Money, Markets and the Future of Higher Education.* London: Verso.

O'Leary, S. (2013) *Dead Student Working.* University of Greenwich unpublished undergraduate dissertation.

Patomaki, H. 2013 *The Great Eurozone Disaster: From Crisis to Global New Deal*, London: Verso.

Polanyi, M. (1958) *Personal Knowledge, towards a Post-Critical Philosophy*. Chicago: University of Chicago Press.

Robbins, D. (1988) *The Rise of Independent Study, The politics and the philosophy of an educational innovation, 1970 – 87.* Buckingham: Open University Press and Society for Research in Higher Education.

Robinson, E. (1968) *The New Polytechnics, The People's Universities*. London: Cornmarket Press.

Silver, R. (2004) *14-19 Reform: The Challenge to HE*, Presentation to Higher Education Policy Institute at the House of Commons 29 June 2004.

Simon, B. (1985) 'Why No Pedagogy in England?' in *Does Education Matter?* London: Lawrence and Wishart.

Spours, K. & Hodgson, A. (2012) *Towards a universal upper secondary education system in England, A unified and ecosystem vision*. London: Institute of Education.

Standing, G. (2011) *The Precariat. The new dangerous class.* London: Bloomsbury.

UNESCO (1997) *Resolution adopted on the report of Commission II at the 26th plenary meeting.* Paris: UNESCO.

Weaver, T. (1974) *Higher than What, Further than Where?* lecture at Rotherham College of Technology.

Weyers, M. & Ainley, P. (2008) 'The variety of student experience, Investigating the complex dynamics of undergraduate learning in "The Times Top 30" and other universities in England' in J. Canaan & W. Shumar (eds) *Structure and Agency in the Neoliberal University* London: Routledge.

Chapter 7

Democratising Local School Systems: Participation and Vision

Richard Hatcher

Introduction

In the three years or so that Michael Gove has been secretary of state for education under the Coalition government he has transformed local school systems. It is a remarkable achievement. It also presents its critics with a challenge. What should a local school system look like? What should be the role of a local authority and its relationship with schools? Who should have a say in local education policy-making, and what structures would best enable it?

In the first section of this chapter I describe the situation that a Labour or Labour-LibDem government is likely to inherit if they are elected in 2015, and situate education in the wider context of local government theory. In the middle section I discuss the position that Labour currently puts forward. In the final section I present some ideas for a democratised local school system. The most radical of Gove's reforms, built on the foundations laid by Labour, has been the spread of academies, currently over half of all secondary schools and approaching ten percent of all primary schools, and likely to continue increasing until 2015. The intended consequence has been the disempowering of local authorities in education. The loss of schools has resulted in a loss of income as academies take with them a disproportionate share of the central support grant. This is compounded by the huge government reduction in local authority budgets. The result has been that local authority central support teams, which supported schools in need and were the authorities' principal instrument for influencing the schools by developing and disseminating good practice and innovation, have been decimated and in many cases virtually disappeared.

It is widely believed that the ultimate aim of the Tories' academies and free schools programme is to allow state-funded schools to be owned and run by private companies for profit. In May last year Michael Gove, giving evidence to the Leveson inquiry into phone hacking, was asked whether he hoped free schools would be able to make profits in a Tory second term. He replied:

> 'It's my belief that we could move to that situation but at the moment it's important to recognise that the free schools movement is succeeding without that element and I think we should cross that bridge when we come to it... There are some of my colleagues in the coalition who are very sceptical of the benefits of profit. I have an open mind.' (*Guardian* 29/5/12).

One sign that running state schools for profit is on the agenda is the arrival in England of companies which run chains of for-profit state schools in Sweden and the US. Kunskapsskolan sponsors four academies. IES, another Swedish chain, has a contract to run Breckland Free School in Suffolk. Two of the leading US for-profit chains, Mosaica and K12, have been approved by the DfE as "lead sponsors' of academies.

To have destroyed so much of the postwar education consensus in three years is an impressive achievement. It invites the question: would a Labour government elected in 2015 pursue progressive educational goals with similar single-minded determination? The Tories have followed Milton Friedman's advice to use a crisis – in this case the financial crisis – as an opportunity for rapid and radical change. And yet, judged against the fundamental strategic objective of having secured by 2015 at least a substantial bridgehead into the state school system by private companies running schools for profit – in David Harvey's terms, an enclosure of the commons, accumulation by dispossession – Michael Gove's counter-revolution has failed. According to Friedman, 'a new administration has some six to nine months in which to achieve major changes' (quoted in Naomi Klein's *The Shock Doctrine* 2007, 7). But it turns out that the privatisation of the school system is a much longer and more difficult task, partly because it would be electorally a vote-loser, partly because it is uncertain whether it would in fact be sufficiently profitable. In contrast to the school system, privatisation of the NHS has proceeded much further: in many ways it is less visible, less tangibly local, less accessible to opposition, than for-profit takeover of a local school; and it has proved very attractive to large companies because the profits are assured and large-scale. So an incoming Labour government in 2015 would not have to deal with an entrenched private schools-for-profit sector. What it would have to deal with as a fundamental issue is the role of local authorities and their relationship with schools.

The changing role of local authorities under the Coalition
The roles that the Coalition government has envisaged for local authorities were spelled out in the 2010 White Paper *The Importance of Teaching*. They would have

'a strong strategic role as champions for parents, families and vulnerable pupils. They will promote educational excellence by ensuring a good supply of high quality places, coordinating admissions and developing their school improvement strategies to support local schools.' (DfE 2010, para 16)

Local authorities have generally retained their role in coordinating admissions, though this can mean little more than acting as an administrative clearing-house. Their capacity to ensure a good supply of high quality school places is limited both by lack of funding and by their lack of power to force academies to expand. The two key issues I want to take up are 'school improvement' and the notion of 'champions'. First, school improvement.

'School improvement'
According to the White Paper, 'it should be clear that the primary responsibility for improvement rests with schools' (para. 22) and that 'our aim should be to create a school system which is more effectively self-improving' (para. 7.4). The perspective of a self-improving school system based on school-to-school support in which local authorities play only a marginal role has been advocated by a number of influential academics who are close to government, most notably by David Hargreaves in a number of publications for what is now called the National College for Teaching and Leadership (Hargreaves 2010; 2011; 2012).

Schools have been involved in local networks for mutual support for many years. But the decline in the capacity of local authorities to directly support schools, coupled with the increased pressure on schools to raise attainment or at least maintain standards (particularly with the advent of forced academisation and the replacement of the Ofsted criterion of 'satisfactory' by 'requiring improvement', which has put thousands more schools at risk of intervention), has led to a qualitative growth of collaboration among schools, ranging from *ad hoc* temporary support (perhaps through permanent new school support alliances) to permanent collaborative structures such as federations. This growth in collaboration has an ambivalent political character. On the one hand, it is a positive development based on a commitment to the wider community of schools – 'collective moral purpose' is the common phrase – rather than just individual competition. On the other hand, it tends to be entirely subject to and limited by the government's school improvement agenda, and may take the form of forced collaboration as a result of a school being taken over as a forced academy by an existing academy.

But the main practical problem with a self-improving school system is that support tends to be patchy and uneven. There are three reasons. One, as Ron Glatter suggests, is the countervailing pressure of competition.

> 'Considerable scepticism should therefore greet attempts to elaborate such laissez-faire approaches, for example David Hargreaves's concept of a "self-improving school system" which is being promoted by the National College for School Leadership, now an executive agency of the Department for Education. As a major OECD review of over 200 studies on introducing markets in school education pointed out, collaboration can be a fragile process in a competitive climate: "[R]esearch from different contexts suggests that cooperation is a vulnerable strategy and requires continuous mutual agreement. Competitive behaviour can be decided on by an individual school and has a tendency to spread with time".' (Glatter 2012, 413-4)

Another reason is the shortage of capacity among schools to offer support to other schools because they are under such pressure themselves to maintain and improve their performance and devoting resources to other schools may put them at risk. But there is also a fundamental design flaw in a self-improving school system: the absence of a local authority capable of identifying and coordinating need and available expertise in the schools.

Present government policy places local authorities in an impossible situation. The lethal cuts in their central support teams mean that local authorities no longer have the capacity to provide much support to schools directly and are largely reliant on brokering support for schools. Yet, extraordinarily, local authorities are held responsible by Ofsted for all schools in their area, including academies and free schools.

> 'Ofsted will inspect the effectiveness of local authority education functions in promoting improvement, high standards and the fulfilment of educational potential of children and young people in schools.' (Ofsted 2013, 11)

The Framework is explicit that this responsibility is not restricted to maintained schools: it covers 'supporting and challenging educational provision in a local authority area' (7). (It has been strongly criticised by the Society of Local Authority Chief Executives and Senior Managers: SOLACE 2013).

In addition to the compulsion from Ofsted, the large majority of local authorities have been reluctant to abandon involvement in their local school system for other reasons: a commitment to the idea of a local schools system which is more than a fragmented aggregation of schools, the desire to link schools to other services and policies of the council, such as social services and safeguarding

131

or economic development, and a sense of local civic identity.

A new partnership between schools and local authorities
Many local authorities have responded to the new situation by constructing a new partnership with local schools which is a new departure in two fundamental respects. First, it is designed to include all the schools in their area, including academies and free schools. This new partnership strategy is based on one positive basic principle: that there is such a thing as a local school system which is more than an aggregation of local schools and which is worth defending. Therefore there needs to be a coordination of provision, including academies and free schools, in the local area covered by the local authority, as against fragmentation. The second innovatory principle is much more contentious. These new partnerships are under the control of headteachers, not the local authority. The local authority is a participant but in a non-voting capacity (similar to Schools Forums).

Two recent research-based studies, one published by the Association of Directors of Children's Services (ADCS 2012; Crossley-Holland 2012), the other by the DfE in association with the Local Government Association (Parish *et al* 2012), contain surveys of a number of authorities which have put this new model in place. A further case in point, not in these reports but typical of them, is Liverpool. In 2012 the Liverpool Learning Partnership was initiated, designed to bring together all the headteachers in the city in a new partnership with the local authority but which is clearly controlled by the headteachers. In July 2013 *From Better to Best*, the report of the Mayor of Liverpool's Education Commission, which was chaired by Estelle Morris, was published. The first recommendation of the report, which is endorsed by the city's headteachers, is that the 'Liverpool Learning Partnership should be acknowledged as the lead agency in the development of the strategic vision for education in the city.' (51)

This is a radical new development. Of course it has long been the case that headteachers, not local authorities, have exercised the power at individual school level. But this is the first time in the nearly a century and a half history of the local authority system that headteachers have been invited to exercise collective control over education policy at authority-wide level. It raises two fundamental questions of education policy at the local level. One is, who should be involved in making local education policy and what influence should they have? The other is, what should local education policy comprise? In short, leadership by who, and leadership for what?

Who should be involved in making local education policy and what influence should they have?

In the new partnerships power lies almost entirely with the headteachers not with the local authority. Decisions are taken by a representative board of heads with one or two local authority representatives (perhaps the Cabinet member for education and a senior officer) present in a non-voting capacity. The question of educational principle is this: why should the development of the strategic vision for education in a local authority be the responsibility principally and almost exclusively of headteachers? What should be the legitimate roles in policy decision-making in the local school system of elected local government and of parents and other stakeholders in the community?

The roles of parents and communities

The new partnerships described in the ADCS and Parish *et al* reports, and those (from my own research) in Liverpool, Bradford and Birmingham, all exclude representatives of parents, teachers and other school staff, local communities, and even school governors. Instead, both reports endorse the 2010 White Paper's conception that 'local authorities have an indispensable role to play as champions of children and parents' (DfE 2010, 34). The term 'champion' in this discourse signifies that the role of the local authority is to speak and act on behalf of children, parents – and communities – but not to enable them to speak and participate in decision-making for themselves. Parents and other key stakeholders are excluded from the partnership, the key local site where policy is discussed and decided. Exploiting democratic legitimacy has only a vacuous rhetorical force in the absence of actual representation of democratically expressed views. The new partnership is a closed managerialist network. The reason is that wider participation – by parents for example – would open the possibility of the partnership becoming a contested space in which managerial and state interests are challenged, putting at risk the partnership project of managing 'school improvement' on behalf of government.

What is at stake here is the relationship between representative democracy and participatory democracy, and specifically fundamental and contested issues of democratic rights in local education policy-making at the authority-wide level, revolving around the politics of voice and the politics of knowledge: whose voices, whose knowledge and what kinds of knowledge count in educational governance.

What should local education policy comprise? Leadership for what?

I turn now from the question of democracy raised by the new partnerships to that of the educational policies that they promote. The term 'vision' frequently occurs in official policy documents about the new role of local authorities. The ADCS report recommends seven key features of the effective future local authority. First is 'An inspiring and inspirational vision and values for the local authority area developed with schools...' (Crossley-Holland 2012 14). Liverpool's Education Commission report is typical of local authority new partnership documents: 'Education should be built on a strong strategic vision for young people and education in the city.' (Mayor of Liverpool's Education Commission 2013, 35)

The question is what sort of 'vision'? The crucial divide is whether the new partnerships restrict themselves to being local relays of the government's performance agenda or attempt to develop and promote a vision and policies for their local school system that go beyond, and put into question, neo-liberal education policy. The ADCS's seven features of effective local authorities essentially accept, and are restricted to, 'official' school improvement and this is typical of its case study local authorities. In some local authority documents there are indications of two additional elements, which can be categorised as enrichment and employability. So, for example, the Liverpool report speaks of an 'Enhanced Curriculum' supported by 'a Pupil Promise which sets out the learning experiences and opportunities the city's schools will offer its pupils' and which 'should go beyond the national curriculum entitlement...' (46). It also states that the curriculum should link to the economic regeneration of the city.' (35).

What is absent is any notion of critical education. I will return to this point, but just to give an example: education for employability can include fostering a critical understanding of the world of work, or it can be in Patricia McCafferty's words (2010, 541), 'the increasingly pervasive embedding of rhetoric and practices of 'enterprising education' as 'an aspect of a 'neoliberal pedagogy'.

We don't yet have any detailed research-based evidence of the policies pursued by the new partnerships, nor of the extent to which headteachers in the new partnerships actually exercise leadership. The ADCS report *The future role of the local authority in education* (Crossley-Holland 2012, 15) urges local authorities, though they lack power, to 'Maximise use of influence to shape the system'. But we don't have evidence of the extent to which local authorities are able to exercise influence over partnership policy decisions, or whether, even if they can, their 'vision' amounts to much more than a lowest common denominator agreement to coordinate support for schools in categories or 'at risk'.

The new partnerships in the local government context

To understand the nature of these new school-local authority partnerships it is useful to situate them in the wider context of developments and debates in the field of local governance theory and policy. The new local education partnerships represent a form of network governance. According to Janet Newman (2004, 71), 'Governance theory starts from the proposition that we are witnessing a shift from government (through direct control) to governance (through steering, influencing, and collaborating with multiple actors in a dispersed system).' Networks 'are the analytic heart of the notion of governance in the study of public administration.' (Rhodes 2000, 60, quoted in Davies 2011, 11). The typical pattern is of horizontal network governance relationships being subordinated to hierarchical control by the state, whether acting within the network or regulating it externally (Davies 2011, 59-60).

In the case of the new education partnerships, control is exercised largely externally by government through the coercive power of the performativity regime, policed by the regulative powers of Ofsted and the DfE and the threat of forced takeover by academy sponsors. However, a recent change in Ofsted gives it a new permanent interventionist role in the new local partnerships by making senior HMIs each proactively responsible for one or several local authorities. The combination of the responsibility of local authorities for school improvement in all the local schools and Ofsted's power to inspect local authorities, together with the well-known pressures they impose on schools, will ensure that the education partnership network is predominantly if not exclusively an instrument and relay of the government's performance agenda through a process of what Bob Jessop calls 'regulated self-regulation' (Jessop 2002, 199).

The coerced acquiescence of local authorities is part of a wider change in the role of local government. According to Colin Copus (2013, 393):

> 'Encouraging public service provision through complex networks has enabled central government to corrode the governing capacity of local government to such an extent that we are left wondering: do we still need elected local government?'

Councils have abandoned their political governing role and now focus just on service delivery, determined by government targets and savagely reduced budgets.

> 'The tendency for councillors to focus on service provision rather than governing (highlights the tensions between the technocratic (managerial) processes and forces and the counteracting political elements. It also highlights the strength of connection between local government as a service-orientated body rather than a governing institution.' (Copus 2013, 396)

What will Labour do?

I have sketched the situation of local school systems which a Labour government would be faced with if it were elected in 2015. What do we know up to now of the response of the Labour leadership?

First, a Labour government would continue with the cuts in local council budgets. Ed Miliband, speaking at Labour's National Policy Forum in Birmingham on 22 June 2013, stressed that 'our starting point for 2015-16 is that we won't be able to reverse the cuts in day to day, current spending unless it is fully funded from savings elsewhere or extra revenue, not from more borrowing.' (quoted on LabourList website)

But the cuts are not the only Coalition policy that Labour would retain. Academies and free schools, the spearhead of the Tories' neoliberal offensive, would continue to exist under a Labour government, as advocated by Lord Adonis, an uncritical supporter of Gove's policy (Adonis 2012), even though there is no evidence that academies do better than local authority schools if you compare like with like (see for example Wrigley and Kalambouka 2012). The most recent statement by Stephen Twigg, Labour's shadow secretary of state for education, is 'No School Left Behind', his speech at the RSA on 17 June 2013.

> 'We need to demonstrate that we put high school standards over and above any dogma regarding school structures. If sponsored academy status is the best solution for a failing school, it should happen.'

Twigg continued:

> 'there will be no bias for or against a school type – so new academies, new maintained schools, new trust schools – all options.'

Free schools will also continue, but rebranded as 'a parent-academy programme to allow parent groups to set up new schools' (Steve Reed MP, Chair of the Parliamentary Labour Party's Education Committee, *Progress Online*, 22 August 2013).

Twigg has made a number of vague statements about the role of local authorities in school improvement but without specifying what powers they would have.

> 'We need stronger local oversight for all schools so that struggling schools are spotted much sooner, local support is on hand to drive up standards, and schools have a clear relationship with their community....we will ensure that every school plays its part to raise standards across their area and meet the needs of their community. Schools working in collaboration. A proven recipe for success. Networked schools in a networked world. No school left behind.' (RSA speech)

Quotable soundbites, but how will it be ensured that 'local support is on hand' and that 'every school plays its part'? Twigg has asked David Blunkett, education secretary 1997-2001 during the Blair government, to lead a review into 'the local oversight of schools', looking at the role of the local authority, when presumably this will be clarified.

One positive step Labour has announced is to allow local authorities to intervene in academies and free schools. According to Reed,

> 'It is critical that we are tough with schools that are failing their pupils – so Labour would introduce new powers to allow local authorities to issue notices to improve for all

schools, including free schools and academies. This will reintroduce local democratic accountability in place of the Tories' centralisation of control in Whitehall' (*ProgressOnline* 22/8/13)

In his chapter in the *Purple Book*, published by Progress in 2012, and disingenuously entitled 'Letting the people decide: redistributing power and renewing democracy', Twigg advocated more power to scrutiny committees, but the idea has not resurfaced since.

> 'Progressives should campaign for local authorities to have more power to scrutinise local providers both within the public and private sector. Councillors should have the legal power to insist bodies and companies give information to scrutiny committees and attend scrutiny meetings.' (Twigg 2012, 277)

Twigg has also made a number of statements on community empowerment, in his 2013 RSA speech:

> '...we will deliver a radical devolution of power from Whitehall. It is not feasible, nor is it desirable, for thousands of schools to be accountable only to the Secretary of State. Local communities will have a greater say about education in their area.'

In an email to *LabourList* on 17 June 2013 Twigg put it more bluntly: 'Key decisions about schooling should be taken in the community.' However, and typically, he did not specify what decisions or how communities would be able to take them.

Several pro-Labour education campaign groups have sought to influence Labour policy as the general election approaches. A comprehensive set of policy proposals was published in 2013 by CASE (the Campaign for State Education), supported by, among others, the SEA (the Socialist Educational Association) and the journal *Forum*, under the title *A Better Future for Our Schools* (available on the CASE website). It rightly notes that 'Opportunities for local communities to have any influence over their local school system are being diminished and decision-making is being concentrated in the DfE.' and asks 'How can we make Education accountable to local communities?' Its answer is to

> 'Establish clear responsibilities for local authorities in planning, commissioning and monitoring of all schools in their area; Ensure that local communities are empowered to play an active role in the planning, commissioning and monitoring of Education provision in their area.'

These proposals are no more specific, and go no further, than those of Twigg. And, like Twigg, and perhaps as a concession in the hope of influencing him on other issues, the CASE manifesto accepts the continuance of academies and, worse, sponsor chains. It says, 'Place all publicly funded schools within a common administrative and legal framework'. This might be interpreted as meaning that academies and free schools would be fully integrated into the local authority system. But they can't be as long as they are owned and controlled by private sponsors, and the following sentence makes clear that sponsors would still remain with only one limited new constraint:

> 'Require all state funded schools and any linked trusts and sponsors, the DfE and all government agencies to be accountable for their decisions and for the use of public money by complying with freedom of information and publishing data of all kinds.'

Towards a democratic participatory local school system
We are at a critical time. As Goveism becomes increasingly discredited and the general election in 2015 draws nearer, there is a growing sense that we need to seize the opportunity to not just critique the education policies of the present government and its New Labour predecessor but to develop and discuss what an alternative might look like. But there is also a growing concern that the Labour leadership is failing to take advantage of this opportunity by refusing to put forward a coherent and radical set of policies or to engage in serious public and professional debate about alternatives and that, if elected in 2015, it will content itself with limited reforms which ameliorate some of the worst Coalition policies while leaving key elements of Goveism intact.

Finland: empowered local authorities in partnership with schools
Finland is widely regarded on the left as perhaps the most successful progressive school system today. As Andy Hargreaves pointed out in his research report on *School leadership for systemic improvement in Finland* (Hargreaves *et al* 2007), 'One of the main features of educational leadership in Finland, (similar to other Nordic countries following decentralisation) is the strong role played by local municipalities.' Hargreaves' report is worth quoting because it offers a model of how empowered local government and schools can work together.

> 'The more than four hundred municipalities (or, in the case of upper secondary vocational education, their consortia) are the owners of the majority of schools, they finance their schools (to a significant degree from their own revenues) and they are the employers of teachers (including school leaders). Furthermore […] they also play a key role in curriculum planning and development.' (28)

'...principals are responsible for their own schools but also for their districts, and [...] there is shared management and supervision as well as evaluation and development of education planning. [...] These reforms are seen as a way to align schools and municipalities to think systemically with the key objective of promoting a common schooling vision and a united school system.' (5)

'Helsinki, for example, is setting a new vision for 2012 (with benchmarks after three years) with every school discussing what the vision along with desired objectives might mean for them.' (13)

'Redistributing leadership within the municipality, between municipal authorities and schools, between schools and within schools, all at the same time, significantly changes the way leadership functions throughout the local system. [...] In this new web of horizontal and vertical interdependence, new behaviours also emerge. Principals start to consider and address broader community needs rather than competitively defending the interests of their own organisation.' (28)

The re-creation of an all-inclusive local school system

Finland provides an example of a national system of inclusive local school systems governed by empowered local authorities in partnership with schools. A similar approach in England would require three major changes of national government policy. (Of course, these are not the only changes that a Labour government should make.)

First, the re-creation of fully inclusive local systems of state-funded schools by the re-integration of academies and the integration of free schools, and an end to private sponsor chains. No state-funded schools should be 'sponsored' or controlled by private organisations. (This is not intended to affect denominational schools, which is a separate argument.) David Wolfe, the education legal expert, has demonstrated that funding agreements can be overridden (Wolfe 2013). Governing bodies of schools which were previously academies should be re-formed to ensure that they have the same composition as maintained schools. If a school wants to continue a partnership with an ex-sponsor, as with any external organisation, it should be able to do so, but this does not require any power to be handed over to it from the reconstituted governing body – and let's see how many of these millionaires and over-paid officials who run chains of academies retain their enthusiasm for education when they are asked to support schools but not control them!

Second, local authorities need power and resources. The most obvious examples are the control of admissions policy and the provision of school places. But they also need the capacity in terms of powers and resources to support schools in addressing problems and to intervene effectively in schools which are under-performing, principally by initiating, coordinating and funding collaborative school partnerships for improvement with more successful schools.

They also need the capacity to promote progressive pedagogic and curriculum innovation. Local authorities have to be able to restrict the exercise of school autonomy if it conflicts with wider community interests in social justice – by for example pursuing polices which serve to disadvantage other schools – through dialogue if possible but with reserve powers if necessary. And of course a re-empowered local authority requires an end to the massive cuts imposed by central government.

And third, local school systems need freeing from the tyranny of

Ofsted, which needs replacing by a rigorous and supportive inspection system, perhaps of headteachers and local authority officers with external moderation, as an integral element of an authority-wide 'school improvement' strategy.

'School improvement' is now largely the responsibility of the schools themselves, supporting each other when needed. But without central coordination it can be patchy, uneven. Some schools are left behind. So there is a vital role for the local authority in identifying schools which need additional support, coordinating provision, and providing direction.

But the role of the local authority has to go beyond supporting schools in difficulties and raising test and exam scores to promoting a local vision for all schools, developed in a dialogue with schools and communities. An education that inspires children and young people with a love of learning and enables them to gain the knowledge, skills and values to make the world a better place, and can effectively challenge the massive social inequalities in the school system. There is a history of local authorities playing an important role of visionary educational leadership: Alec Clegg in the West Riding 1945-74, a pioneer of creative child-centred teaching and the role of the arts; Leicestershire under Stewart Mason from the late 1950s through to the 1970s, a pioneer of comprehensive schools with progressive teaching and internal democratic regimes; the ILEA from 1965-1990 developing policies to tackle inequalities of 'race' and gender; Birmingham's enriched experiential curriculum under Tim Brighouse 1993-2002.

Today's context requires both building on and radicalising this tradition. Michael Fielding and Peter Moss (2011) in their book *Radical Education and the Common School: A democratic alternative*, say that

> 'The radical traditions with which we identify are those
> which reject the presumptions and aspirations not just of
> neoliberal forms of capitalism, but much of what capitalism
> itself stands for... We would wish to support radical
> approaches to practice that [...] call into question the moral
> and existential basis of acquisitive consumerism and
> economism...' (151)

They envisage the role of the local authority 'as a leader and
facilitator of the development of a local educational project, a
shared and democratic exploration of the meaning and practice of
education and the potential of the school.' (125) They propose four
imperatives as the basis of the curriculum.

> 'The first is a focus on the purposes of education, organising
> the curriculum around that which is necessary for a
> sustainable, flourishing and democratic way of life. The
> second has to do with equipping young people and adults
> with the desire and capacity to seriously and critically
> interrogate what is given and co-construct a knowledge that
> assists us in leading good and joyful lives together. The third
> argues that while knowledge must transcend the local, it
> must, nonetheless, start with the cultures, concerns and hopes
> of the communities that the school serves. (81)

Fourth is a curriculum that emphasises connectedness.

For Fielding and Moss, 'the development of radical education and
the common school needs to go hand-in-hand with the renewal and
development of democratic local government, which in our view
has to include an active and innovative role in education.' (127)
The democratisation of local government in England requires not

only a new partnership with schools in which the local authority plays a leading role in service provision, it also requires, as Colin Copus argues, a revival of the democratic role of local councils, in terms both of representative and participatory democracy. Councils need

> '...to move beyond a focus solely on public services to a role which stresses the capacity of local government to control, shape and direct the local political environment and the local state (Cockburn 1977). To do that local government has to be conceptualised as having a governing role within the overall political system. That role requires debates about local government to stress the political and governing elements rather than service provision, so that the development of a normative model of local government democracy is one which sees citizens as political actors (passive or active) and links this to the governing, policy-development and representative role of local government. [...]
>
> 'The political aspect of local government however, extends beyond the frontiers of representative democracy and the processes associated with it into a more comprehensive democratic contribution. Local government provides a framework within which greater variety of policy and political contributions can be made – both representative and participatory in nature.' (Copus 2013, 394)

The basic principle is this: every citizen has a stake in, and therefore should have a say in, their local school system as well as their local school. Potentially the most powerful source of support at the local level for more progressive and egalitarian education policies by schools and local authorities is pressure for them from parents and communities, and the most effective strategy for developing and mobilising it is their participation in local education policy-making, but this is precisely what is ruled out by their deliberate exclusion by headteachers and local authorities from the new managerial partnerships they are currently constructing. As Andy Hargreaves and Dennis Shirley (2009) argue, in 'a resilient social democracy' (107):

> 'Community organizing in education goes far beyond parent involvement and its traditional one-on-one deals between individual parents and the educators who serve their children. It is about mobilizing entire communities and public networks to agitate for significant reform. When fully realized, it is about changing the power dynamics of an entire city by creating new civic capacity for previously disenfranchised populations.' (59)

There is a rich tradition of community organising for education in the US: see the examples in Hargreaves and Shirley's book (60-62) and also in books by Jean Anyon (2005) and Pauline Lipman (2011). The closest example in England in the last decade is local anti-academy campaigns. But campaigns are generally temporary. They need to be complemented by institutional forms which enable permanent popular participation. I would suggest there are three:

- Opening up the authority-wide Partnerships to popular participation

- The creation of Local Education Forums

- Democratisation of the structures and procedures of the local authority

Participation in the Partnership
The authority-wide Partnerships between schools – actually, headteachers – and local authorities need to be opened up to

participation by parents, teachers, support staff, other professionals, school governors, and members and representatives of the local community, so they can come together to discuss and take positions on key issues of education policy and practice. This could take a number of forms: perhaps a public authority-wide Education Forum which elected representatives to the Partnership board. This would be a radical democratic innovation, though it would be the logic of the aspirations that Stephen Twigg has voiced.

One small step in this direction is Bradford's Public Forum for Education. This is an open forum meeting five times a year where everyone, including parents and carers, young people and professionals, is welcome to come along and contribute. Senior councillors and officers join the debates, listen to views, and report back to the Forum what action they have taken as a result. The next step towards democratisation would be to link the Forum structurally, through elected representatives, to Bradford's Education Improvement Strategic Board, which was established to oversee the development and implementation of the Council's policies and comprises councillors, officers, headteachers and governors and the Leader of the Council as chair.

Local Education Forums
Increasingly local school systems are being organised into groups of schools, in clusters and networks, cooperating together to serve a local area, perhaps as small as a neighbourhood, perhaps the size of a town. There needs to be a body – we can call it a Local Education Forum – which brings together parents, local residents and community organisations, together with staff and school students. Its purposes would be two-fold. One, to harness the energy and expertise and enthusiasm of the community to enrich learning in the local schools and build the culture of a local learning

community.   Two, to enable the community, as a stakeholder, to participate in local education policy-making along with the professionals. It would also elect representatives to the authority-wide Partnership.

Democratisation of the structures and procedures of the local authority

Public participation in discussion of education policy is meaningless without the ability to influence local authority policy. The local authority would need to resource, actively promote, and engage with the Forums. But the existing structures and processes of local government – the Cabinet and Scrutiny system – also need to be opened up to popular and professional participation. At present they are largely immune to any direct involvement by headteachers, teachers and governors, let alone parents and other citizens. There are two key measures needed to democratise the present structures. First, the Education Scrutiny Committee should be opened up to representation and input from the Partnership and from the Local Education Forums.

Second the local council should establish an Education Committee. The Cabinet system which replaced Council Committees was introduced into local government by Blair in 1997 in order to centralise power and enable faster decision-making. The result has been a profound democratic deficit as power is monopolised by a small minority of councillors. The previous Committee system – which is still legal and which some councils still use – has two major advantages. First, it means that far more councillors are involved in policy-making. At present, Cabinet members responsible for service areas have no committee of colleagues to work with, leaving them isolated and too dependent on officers. Second, and crucial from the point of view of participatory democracy, council committees can co-opt lay members onto the committees and sub-committees. This was common practice among especially the more radical Labour Councils in the 1970s and 80s, where the co-opted members were often elected by various groups as their representatives, with voice though without vote. It was an important factor in the effectiveness of these Councils in tackling issues of gender and ethnic equality. This is exactly what is needed today to tackle the key issues that councils face in education. These committees could be set up now, even with the Cabinet system in place. There is nothing to stop the Cabinet member for education from setting up an advisory committee with other councillors on it and inviting the local education Partnership to elect representatives to it.

Of course, democratic participation in the formation of local authority policy without the ability to translate policy from the local authority level to the school level, and to intervene on key issues if dialogue fails, is pointless. It has to be recognised that for the schools this is a very sensitive and contentious issue. The existing and emerging Partnership model is controlled by headteachers. Why should they agree to handing power back to the local authority, and in particular one which is itself subject to popular participation and pressure? Schools may be reluctant to concede local authority influence over anything more than admissions policy and the provision of school places. The only way that schools could be persuaded to accept this new settlement is if in return they felt confident that they could have a meaningful influence in co-constructing local authority policy, through the Partnership, through a participative Education Committee (Bradford's Strategic Education Board is a step in that direction) and through a reconstructed Scrutiny Committee.

Public participation in policy-making in local schools systems does not mean intervening in issues which are properly matters of professional judgement. Nor does it imply that public views are inevitably progressive. In both cases it is a question of deliberation and negotiation between, and among, public and professionals, and the mobilisation of collective popular and professional support for progressive policies.

References

Association of Directors of Children's Services (2012) *The Missing Link: The evolving role of the local authority in school improvement.* London: ADCS.

Adonis, A. (2012) *Education, Education, Education.* London: Biteback Publishing.

Anyon, J. (2005) *Radical possibilities.* London: Routledge.

Copus, C. (2013) 'Repoliticising local democracy'. *Policy & Politics* 43 (3) 389-408.

Crossley-Holland, J. (2012) *The future role of the local authority in education.* London: ADCS.

Davies, J.S. (2011) *Challenging governance theory: From networks to hegemony.* Bristol: Policy Press.

Department for Education (2010) *The importance of Teaching.* London: HMSO.

Fielding, M. & Moss, P. (2011) *Radical Education and the*

Common School: a democratic alternative. London: Routledge.

Glatter, R. (2010) 'Towards Whole System Improvement'. *Forum* 54: 3, 411-6.

Hargreaves, D.H. (2012) *A self-improving school system: towards maturity.* Nottingham: National College for School Leadership.

Hargreaves, D.H. (2011) *Leading a self-improving school system.* Nottingham: National College for School Leadership.

Hargreaves, D.H. (2010) *Creating a self-improving school system.* Nottingham: National College for School Leadership.

Hargreaves, A., Halasz, G. & Pont, B. (2007) *School leadership for systemic improvement in Finland.* Paris: Organization for Economic Cooperation and Development.

Hargreaves, A. & Shirley, D. (2009) *The Fourth Way.* London: Corwin.

Jessop, B. (2002) *The future of the capitalist state.* Cambridge: Polity Press.

Klein, N. (2007) *The Shock Doctrine. The Rise of Disaster Capitalism.* London: Penguin
Lipman, P. (2011) *The new political economy of urban education.* London: Routledge.

Mayor of Liverpool's Education Commission (2013) *From Better to Best.* Liverpool: Liverpool City Council.

McCafferty, P. (2010) 'Forging a "neoliberal pedagogy": The "enterprising education" agenda in schools'. *Critical Social Policy* 30: 4, 541-563.

Newman, J. (2004) Modernizing the state: a new form of governance? in J. Lewis & R. Surender (eds) *Welfare state change: towards a third way?* Oxford: Oxford University Press.

Ofsted (2013) *The framework for the inspection of local authority arrangements for supporting school improvement.* Manchester: Ofsted.

Parish, N., Baxter, A. & Sandals, L. (2012) *Action research into the evolving role of the local authority in education. The final report for the Ministerial Advisory Group.* London: DfE. (Research Report DFE-RR224)

Rhodes, R.A.W. (2000) 'The governance narrative: key findings and lessons from the ESRC's Whitehall programme'. *Public Administration* 78:2, 345-63.

SOLACE (Society of Local Authority Chief Executives and Senior Managers) (2013) *SOLACE Statement on New Ofsted Inspection Framework for Local Authorities.* 15 May. Available at http://www.solace.org.uk/press/Statement_on_New_Ofsted_Inspection_Framework_for_Local_Authorities/

Twigg, S. (2012) 'Letting the people decide: redistributing power and renewing democracy'. In R. Philpot (ed) *The Purple Book*. London: Biteback Publishing.

Wolfe, D. (2013) Schools: 'The Legal Structures, the Accidents of History and the Legacies of Timing and Circumstance'. *Education Law Journal*, May. Available on his canofworms website. (See also the notes on his presentation at the 'Picking Up the Pieces' CASE conference in November 2012 (www.campaignforstateeducation.org.uk/DavidWolfe.html)

Wrigley, T. & Kalambouka, A. (2012) *Academies and achievement: setting the record straight*. Available at www.changingschools.org.uk.

Chapter 8

The Long Counter-Revolution

Ken Jones

Introduction

The education policy of the Coalition, which is largely the education policy of the Conservative Party, is to an important extent conceived politically. That is to say, its efforts to steer the education system through the various problems presented by economic crisis and social change are always intertwined with the attempt to outmanoeuvre and defeat those who might oppose it. Politics is not only a matter of the day-to-day business of parliamentary affairs; so far as Conservatism is concerned, it is also the attempt to achieve a decisive set of transformations that remove from the scene institutions and social actors which have been central to education for more than a hundred years and to assert new goals, new institutions, new patterns of social relations within the system. Politics in these senses is strongly antagonistic and is pursued with long-term change in mind.

This is why Michael Gove talks so much about the past, insisting that the undead forces of 1980s progressivism must finally be killed off. It is why he is so hyperbolically combative in his utterances, so despotic in his manner of decision-making. Gove is not a traditionalist, if that means that he would want education to return to some idealised former state: he is committed to a school system fit for a neo-liberal world, of sharp social inequalities, and a stratified labour market. But in other senses, his affinity with conservative tradition is strong. As Corey Robin (2011) points out, conservatism has always been constituted by its struggle against the left; Michael Gove, like Salisbury, or Thatcher, can be understood in this frame. He sees himself as dealing with a mortal threat to principles that Conservatives think are essential to any social order – competition, selectivity, hierarchy and the notions of quality and excellence that legitimate the inequalities that they entail. These principles were placed in danger by the direction of social, political and educational change in the later twentieth century. The 1988 Education Reform Act, and much that has happened since, have held the danger in check, but it has not been completely removed. Teacher trade unions, local councils, university departments of education all retain an influence that affects the ambiance of schooling, inflecting it towards values of inclusiveness, child-centredness and creativity that, however weakly embedded, must be removed from the scene. Gove's policies, like his rhetoric, are driven by this purpose: they are aimed at identifying, contesting and defeating ideas and practices which carry the traces of a different educational project. It is in this sense that one can speak of 'counter-revolution' as a defining feature of his programme: it is this that links him to Edmund Burke.

If Gove is a counter-revolutionary, where is the 'revolution' to which he is reacting? Here we encounter one of the peculiarities of neo-liberal society. The enemy that Conservatives attack (and in attacking, justify their own policies) belongs, in an important sense, to the past. It may have an ideological afterlife, but as a political force capable of shaping institutions and practices it is much weaker than it used to be. Moreover, in its present-day manifestation, the Party which oversaw the most energetic years of educational reform has no interest in contesting the offensive that has been launched against it. Neither Conservatism's historical sense, nor its openly antagonistic policies, are shared by the Labour Party. Along with its acceptance of the ERA framework, Labour has adopted an amnesiac position on the period of reform that followed the 1944 Education Act and reached its peak in the 1970s and 1980s. 1988, for New Labour, was the year zero of educational history (Jones 2004). Nothing before then is useful to retrieve. 'Leave the battles of the past,' Tony Blair told his Party Conference in 1995, and this advice has been followed for nearly two decades. Unwilling to revisit the projects of comprehensive reform and progressive change at classroom level that were pursued before 1988, Labour has no perspective in which to understand Conservative politics, and the stakes that they involve. The speeches of the Shadow Minister, Stephen Twigg, suggest that Conservative policy innovations will be left in place; no fundamental changes are necessary (Twigg 2013). Labour thus has two, equally unappealing, functions in current educational debate: it is the mute object of Conservative misrepresentations of the past; and it is the quiet accompanist of the policy that Conservatives are unrolling into the future.

The Labour Party's lack of commitment to radical educational change, and its lack of interest in taking the measure of Conservative ambitions, may not be unexpected. But they are nonetheless a problem for the 'world of education', that is for many of the interests which, historically, had looked to the Party to provide a national policy framework that provide an environment in which their concerns and aspirations could flourish. Even without such a framework, there is still much oppositional activity. Parents and local authorities have opposed free schools and the policy of forcing allegedly underperforming schools to become academies. A number of pressure groups – the Local Schools

Network, CASE, the Socialist Education Association – make forceful critiques of the Coalition's programme and sketch alternatives to it. Educationalists have attacked Gove's curriculum policies and the testing regime that accompanies them (e.g. Paton 2013). Trade unions have taken action over pay, conditions, pensions and academisation. The student movement of 2010 rose up against the hike in tuition fees. These responses, however, are not strongly inter-related. The mobilisation of thousands of teachers in a campaign over pay and conditions could have provided an occasion to push broader educational issues into the public domain, but this is not an opportunity that has been taken. Conversely, pressure groups are concerned that trade union action will provide Gove with a further justification for policies that rest on central control, and so keep their distance from union-based combativity. Think-tanks of the centre-left, pragmatically calculating the limits of the possible, suggest policy directions that take the achievements of conservatism, such as the hyper-extension of academies, as the starting-points for reform, rather than as obstacles to be removed. The overall picture of the world of education thus certainly includes discontent with the whole range of Coalition policy, but also in its frame is a fragmentation and uncertainty of response that leaves initiative in the hands of the right.

The purpose of this article is to sketch some notes towards an educational strategy that starts from the current impasse of the 'left' – a term I use to mean the dispersed collection of organisations and individuals who oppose the fundamental direction of government education policy, in the name of principles of equality, democracy and educational creativity. The brush it uses is a broad one and the sketch it offers is political as much as policy orientated. Its perspective is long-term, considering present-day issues in the light of education politics since 1945. It tries to focus on education in the context of social and economic change, including change in labour market patterns. It is concerned with the ideologies and agenda of social actors – the groups and movements that try to set the direction of educational change – rather than on the detail of their proposals. Since it aims to be strategic, it tries to indicate issues and locations where the left can most productively apply its energies if it is to turn around the system in which education in England has become embedded. The analysis it offers, which identifies the ways in which austerity and market logic are forces that are restructuring all aspects of education, from early years pedagogy to the work of lecturers in universities, is intended to suggest common themes around which opposition can regroup.

Crisis and Restructuring

The British left in the 1970s was well aware that the onset of recession in the middle of that decade would be utilised not only to justify cuts in social spending but also a restructuring of provision and an attempt to align it with new economic priorities (Weekend Return Group 1980). Thatcherism was the political force that answered to this prediction. It provided Conservatives in the twenty-first century with an example they have been quick to learn from: crisis presents political opportunities to parties that are able to take decisive action. For Marxists, the recession of 2008 was quickly seen as a vindication of their analysis: a system based on debt-fuelled consumption was a crash waiting to happen. For Keynesians, the public bail-outs of the banking sector demonstrated the failings of an unregulated market, and seemed to reassert the state's role as an economic actor (Gamble 2009). But neither of these readings was able to impose itself on the politics of the crisis. The dominant reading came to be that of the right, supported by international financial institutions to be sure, and best articulated by the post-2010 Conservative-led government, which developed both a discourse and a programme of action that had immediate effects, and long-term consequences.

Clarke and Newman point out that the locus of the crisis has been shifted, discursively, from the private to the public sector, from the financial services industry to public spending:

> 'it has been ideologically reworked, at least in the UK, from an economic problem (how to 'rescue' the banks and restore market stability) to a political problem (how to allocate blame and responsibility for the crisis): a reworking that has focused on the unwieldy and expensive welfare state and public sector, rather than high risk strategies of banks, as the root cause of the crisis.' (Clarke and Newman 2012: 303).

On this accepted ground, the government has been able to introduce a programme of cuts and welfare restructuring. Some of the educational consequences are obvious: the loss of the Educational Maintenance Allowance, the cuts to Sure Start. Others will reveal their meaning only over a longer period.

In his classic book *The Three Worlds of Welfare Capitalism*, Gøsta Esping-Andersen discussed the role of welfare states, particularly in the post-war period, in creating a space of 'decommodification'. Relatively generous social security arrangements, along with publicly provided housing, health and childcare meant that in some countries the pressure on workers to accept low wages and make short-term employment choices was reduced. As a result, the economic bargaining power of workers, as individuals, and as a class, was increased. Decommodification, it could be argued, was also a feature of the way that social provision was organised. Schools, for instance, were in some ways distanced

161

from immediate labour market demands, developing cultures where other objectives than economic ones could be pursued. The changes brought about by Thatcherism reduced the space of decommodification by means of a market logic of competitiveness between and within institutions. The development under New Labour of management cultures that drove schools towards higher levels of performance on the basis of narrowly defined indicators consolidated the idea that schools should operate as if they were businesses, with values that in their acceptance of competitive pressures, were strongly commodified. Thus, between 1988 and 2010, the decommodified space identified by Esping-Andersen was greatly reduced. Coalition policies reduce it further.

Three themes of Conservative policy

Conservatives note that there has been no strong challenge to their argument that economic necessity demands cuts in social spending. They go on, therefore, to apply the same logic to social and educational restructuring. The reforms of the Coalition government are intended to push education further along the road to a situation where market logic presses even more heavily on teachers' work and students' learning. This pressure takes three forms.

The first, discussed in Richard Hatcher's chapter in this book, is to multiply the number of schools that are run outside local authority influence, by autonomous managements accountable to central government and to the quasi-market of parental choice. From a Conservative point of view, a school 'system' based on autonomy does not need a workforce that is paid on a nationally-determined basis that school managements cannot control. Though the Labour governments of 1997-2010 made incremental salary progression conditional upon successful passage through a threshold assessment, they left intact the national pay structure, which set out a pattern of incremental progression that all teachers would follow. Michael Gove regards this structure as a relic of the collectivist period. He proposes that individual school managements should be able to set differential pay levels for each teacher, and that, in the case of some categories of schools, they should be able to recruit unqualified teachers. This would have several linked effects on teachers. The recruitment of unqualified staff would downgrade the status of educational knowledge: teachers would be employed for their subject expertise; as for 'the rest' – pedagogy, for instance – this could be picked up on the job. The further reduction in the importance of the pay structure would tend to reduce whatever element of individual professional autonomy teachers still possessed, as well as reducing the element of common ground between teachers in a school. The resulting decollectivisation of the workforce would make it a more effective instrument for the transmission of official educational agenda: the more fragmented the teaching force, the more malleable.

The third kind of pressure falls on students. Gove stands for an educational order that is based on competition between students for a restricted number of prizes. In a speech at Cambridge in 2011 he illustrated what this principle meant in practice:

'In Burlington Danes, an Academy run by the charity ARK in White City, academic excellence is recognised with a rank order system for every pupil in every year, allocating a place to every child in every term based on their performance subject by subject. So at half term the children are examined, given their scores from 1 to 120. That's kept private. Then they have the opportunity in the remaining half term to improve their scores and at the end of it every student in every year is ranked, in every subject and for effort, and also artistic and sporting achievement. When I encountered this the first time I thought – that's a bit hard core, must be unpopular with some of the parents and some of the students. But actually I was told that this had been the single most popular change that had been initiated. The children were now so anxious to do well in this competitive process, which rewards the acquisition of knowledge, that they petition the head to have them transferred out of classes where teachers are weak into those where teaching is strong.' (Gove 2011)

Thatcher, famously, said that the purpose of her policies was to 'change the soul' (Thatcher 1981). We can see in Gove's description how this project works: not so much through exhortation, as through the setting up of a system whose logic induces conformity to market-shaped systems of action. Success in this system is measured positionally, in terms of rank order, with 'excellence' in terms of test results, being a by-product of competitiveness.

In Gove's policies for assessment and public exams, we can see how 'intra-school' processes of this kind are geared to market logics in the world outside the school. As Nico Hirtt has noted (2013), the analyses of CEDEFOP – the EU organisation that focuses on vocational education – confirm what theorists like Castells (2000) were claiming more than a decade ago. The labour-market is sharply divided: 'most job growth will be in higher- and lower-skill occupations with slower growth in occupations requiring medium-level qualifications.' (CEDEFOP 2012, 29) The DfE has introduced a number of changes that point in the direction of a selectivity which matches this pattern of job distribution. Their effect will be to identify at a relatively early stage students capable of competing for higher-skilled jobs, while insisting that passage through formal examination systems at all age levels of schooling, including early years provision (Paton *ibid*), is essential for participation in the labour market. Thus, it is no surprise that a kind of norm-referenced assessment has been introduced in post-16 exams, recreating a *numerus clausus* system so far as the highest grades are concerned (Mansell 2012). At 18+ end-of-term examination has been revived, at the expense of a modular system, and is likely to have similar class-linked effects. The DfE's requirement that schools report their success in terms of the number of their students who gain places at a small group of elite universities (Parr 2013) also encourages a focusing of resources on a privileged layer.

Political effects of restructuring

When Gove took office in 2010, he took over a system that, even if it had been inflected under Labour towards concerns for social inclusion, had been ordered for more than two decades according to an original Conservative plan. He has been able to build on this, strengthening existing tendencies, rather than bringing new ones into being. The cumulative effect of successive policy developments, with the earlier stages providing the grounds for the success of later policies, has made Conservatism a dominant force. Moreover, the balance of power in the political field of education allowed Gove great scope for initiative. After 2010, Labour continued to think within the parameters of neo-liberal orthodoxy and did not see its role as to present an opposition to Gove of any comprehensive sort. Local authorities had lost political authority as well as control over day-to-day policy. A generation of teachers had grown up knowing only the procedures and objectives of the post-1988 system. Parents and students, in social conditions of ever-greater insecurity, were focused on issues of school choice and examination success (Jones 2014a). In this landscape of preoccupation, regulation and political setback, Conservatism was the decisive political force.

From the point of view of the left, this situation represents a defeat of historical significance. In *The Long Revolution* (1961) Raymond Williams showed that the achievements and potential of the socialist movement in Britain depended on interlinked actions and struggles in several different fields. The first was economic. The development of an industrial economy, in the context of working-class struggles that forced it into a welfarist shape, improved the condition of the majority of people – their material prosperity, security, dignity and power. The second revolution was political. Williams, as Michael Rustin emphasises, 'saw the rise of democracy as primarily the practical achievement of the working-class movement' and 'thus linked the struggle for democratisation to a profound change in the balance of power of social classes' (2007, 16). The third aspect of the long revolution was cultural: Williams had a vision of a 'common culture' in which all could participate, a culture enabled in part by a democratised education system, with a curriculum reshaped to match this new task. The three facets of the long-revolutionary process were not, Williams insisted, idealised construction, but had already been actualised in the work of social movements. His book was an attempt to give a name and a meaning to this work, and in doing so extend it.

It is sobering to consider how these processes have fared in the neo-liberal era and dismaying to think about the wreckage of the political projects that were connected to them. Working-class power at the economic level, which set limits to what the capitalist class thought politically feasible, has been severely reduced. Democratic institutions created or shaped by working-class and social movement activity – trade unions and local government; the diverse projects associated with feminism, and black and community movements after 1968 – have been hollowed out or swept away.

In education, likewise, the processes that Williams associated with the long revolution have been checked. For nearly a hundred years, educators concerned with issues of social justice and self-realisation were able to develop these commitments within a state education that to some extent accommodated them. The landmark government reports of the twentieth century register the impact of this engagement. From Hadow in 1926, to Bullock in 1975 – even in later products such as the 1999 report on culture and creativity, *All Our Futures* – policy yoked together a concern for social control and economic productiveness with a different sort of emphasis, from which issues of social justice, equality and individual self-realisation were not absent. At grassroots level, the attempt to establish elements of a common culture was especially strong from the later sixties onwards, when the selection-based insufficiencies of the 1944 Act were criticised, and alternatives developed. Movements for educational change existed on several levels, from the classroom and the school to the local authority and national politics. Owing much to earlier, progressive traditions, they were refuelled by the energies that sprang from political movements in the late sixties. In terms of public debate, it was here that the readiest answers were found to questions of educational practice and purpose. The answers, of course, were ambivalent: it was claimed that a progressivist approach to curriculum reform was not only necessitated by social justice but demanded by a modern economy, as if both forces pulled in the same direction: 'we can afford free men, and we need them' wrote one educationalist (James 1973). Nevertheless, the effect of such ambivalence was that tensions between the economic and the educational were deferred. This for a period allowed space to projects whose objectives and procedures were far from being economistic and which enabled a connection between education and other elements in the long revolutionary process that Williams identified. One way of reading James Callaghan's famous 1976 Ruskin speech is to see it as a call to reassert the primacy of education's economic role, against the practices and ideologies that schooling had become home to.

Current circumstances are different. The difference has partly to do with a reassertion of education's economic purpose and partly to do with a reduction in the autonomy of educational practice. At the same time the lines of connection – intellectual and practical – between education and those spaces in which a democratic common culture might be generated have become more tenuous. To borrow from Gramsci – in a way that I have done in other recent work – much more has occurred here than a mere turnaround of policy; it is not only educational programmes that have been changed, but the entire 'social complex' of relationships and institutions through which such programmes can be imagined, elaborated and realised (Gramsci 1971, 36; Jones 2013).

Responding
There is much to be learned from the right: from Hayek and the Mont Pélerin Society about the long-term development of alternative ideas and programmes; from the Black Papers and the think-tanks of the 70s and 80s about simplicity and concreteness of argument; from Kenneth Baker and Michael Gove about adversarial politics and decisiveness in action. Conservatives have been good at finding points of intervention – issues, real and imaginary, in which the problems of a system are dramatised and

condensed. The image of the red teacher, or the negligent local authority, was used to good effect in the long prologue of mediatised scandal that led up to the ERA (School Without Walls 1978). But there are other things the left has to learn for itself. Unlike the right, it cannot rely on an endlessly supportive media. Nor does it expect or want to achieve change through capture of the existing state apparatus: it cannot managerialise its way to a democratic education and a common culture. Trying to open up the education system to new possibilities is something to be achieved through mobilisation, as well as through legislation and policy change. For the left, therefore, things are harder. Moving people to action is more difficult than constructing a media event. Even so, there are points at which campaigns against immediate injustices give an opportunity to probe longer-term problems of the post-1988 system, on all of the fronts sketched by Williams.

Durkheim suggested that culture and politics are closely related in the work of the school, as subjectivities are linked to a social order. Likewise, economic life, in the form of the social division of labour, has a formative effect on curricula, assessment and selection. To call into question educational practices is thus, in some circumstances, to head in the direction of criticising more general principles of social organisation. The ongoing debate about creativity and its suppression in the post-1988 school has the potential to do this. In the debate's latest phase, specialists in Early Education have counted the cost to children of incessant high stakes testing. Responding to their concerns, Gove has been characteristically dismissive. The under-fives, like everyone else, should be exposed to a:

> 'system that aims to prepare pupils to solve hard problems in calculus or be a poet or engineer – a system freed from the grip of those who bleat bogus pop-psychology about "self

image", which is an excuse for not teaching poor children how to add up.' (Paton 2013)

But this kind of aggressive apologia encounters increasing opposition, particularly in nursery and primary schools. It is a site of conflict that is also a point of vulnerability. The Labour government tried in some sort to defuse the conflict, through a part-espousal of a 'creativity agenda'. Conservatism appears to have no such intention, and is vulnerable for this reason. It should be possible to mobilise against it an alliance of teachers, educationalists and parents that draws strength from a humanist, constructivist tradition with a more generous vision of educational possibility. Beyond confrontations over immediate issues of curriculum and assessment lies the potential for a long-term war of position around education's purposes and practice.

A second area of potential weakness is the government's policy towards teachers, who are still regarded as a threat to educational progress. Inspection, performance management, differential pay and limited autonomy create grounds for conflict between government, school managers and teachers. This conflict is likely to be enduring, since the entire model of school change that government has worked with since the 1990s implies a teaching force that is made pliant by managerialism – a strategy that cuts against teachers' sense of their own professionalism and dignity. The experience of teachers, in this sense, could be constructed, though it isn't currently, as typical of a wider working population, confined within the discipline imposed by neo-liberalism. To present the politics of the educational workplace in these terms, could raise questions of democracy of the sort that Williams raised, but have since been silenced.

The third area of potential weakness concerns the relationship between education and the labour market. Across Europe, youth unemployment is high, and is likely to remain so even when recession ends. Precarity, in the form of low-wage, short-term, part-time employment, is likewise endemic (Standing 2011). The linkage between an education system that demands high performance from all and a labour market that can promise only uncertain rewards is not a stable one. The mobilisation of precarious youth, in part provoked by tensions between education and labour markets, has been a feature of politics across Europe, as well as being strikingly evident in Britain at the start of the Coalition period in 2010-11. It is a mobilisation that is likely to recur; any serious attempt to develop an educational programme of the left will want to relate to it.

Both the analysis offered earlier in this chapter, and the potential areas of conflict listed above, imply that the various different interests in the world of education face problems whose common origin is the neo-liberal turn in education policy that began in the 1980s and which has shaped the experience of parents, students, teachers and educationalists alike. It is essential that a left political programme recognises this and does not proceed on the basis of segregating the apparently separate grievances of different sectors. To do so would be to perpetuate precisely the kinds of division and conflict on which the politics of the right have thrived. A programme that attempts to begin a long revolution must start from a different point, that identifies the afflictions of different sectors and traces them to a common origin. It must also try to identify the themes that can express a shared interest. In this case, it is the development of practices and policies that can so far as possible insulate – 'decommodify' – education, here and now, from market

171

logic, while pointing forward to what can be achieved in the future. Insulation can take the form of strengthened trade unionism, of achieving the abolition of a particular layer of the testing system, of maintaining unstreamed classes and establishing school admissions policies that do not discriminate in favour of already privileged groups. A left programme would insist on the mutual compatibility of such measures; in particular, it would regard trade union action, not as an anachronistic embarrassment, but an essential part of the defence of educational space. Conversely, it would regard as inadequate any trade unionism that did not place the wider politics of education high on its agenda.

Gramsci writes that to be productive the development of a programme – in this context, a set of policies – must be accompanied by a sense of the 'institutions and relationships' that are a necessary part of the programme's realisation. This is likewise the emphasis of *The Long Revolution*: the common culture and the democratic economic and political forms that Williams envisages can only be a collective achievement, an example of mass creativity. For this reason, those attempting to suggest a way forward after a long period of defeat need to think about the social actors whose energies might contribute to reconstruction. In this context, it is impossible not to be struck by the fact that the most creative educational initiatives – those which most squarely address neo-liberal agenda, and try to embody in their practice as well as the content of their discussions, an alternative to it – have arisen outside the formal sector. The 'educational turn' among art workers is one such instance (Rogoff 2010). The post-2010 student movement provides others, about which I have written elsewhere (Jones 2014b). The declaration of the Birmingham Free University exemplifies a more general stand:

'We ... seek to work collectively against the principles that now shape the so-called public university;

'Central to the educational experiences we want to create is the idea that students and teachers have much to learn from one another;

'Thus all who participate in the Birmingham Free University are scholars: student-scholars and teacher-scholars;

'On our courses learning and teaching entail processes of continuous negotiation to ensure the fullest participation of all, recognising, respecting and celebrating human diversity;

'All learning and teaching will be critical – questioning the world as it is to explore how it could be otherwise;

'We believe that in order for all learning and teaching to be critical and democratic, dialogue is essential.

'All critical, democratic dialogue amongst student-scholars and teacher-scholars should, when possible, not just remain in the classroom;

'Thus our ultimate classroom is the wider world; we seek to develop educational processes aiming to build a more socially just and sustainable world.' (Birmingham Free University 2012, original punctuation.)

To read this kind of declaration, and to participate in discussions around it, is to be struck by the thought that the long revolution about which Williams wrote must have had near its beginning statements like this, that looked hard at a situation that had become intolerable and tried to work out a very different way of organising essential human functions, learning and teaching among them. A similar kind of rethinking and (re)discovery has to go into a programme of the left, so that educational ideas and senses of political possibility which have been formed in harsh and depressing contexts can be enriched by other kinds of understanding and commitment. Such an attempt at political alliance, and intellectual synthesis, is essential to confronting a situation whose logic is institutionally embedded, and opponents who, despite the conflicts and tensions of their own programme, remain politically resourceful and ideologically fluent.

References

Birmingham Free University (2012)
http://www.indymedia.org.uk/en/2012/03/494226.html

Castells, M. (2000) *End of Millennium, Volume III: The Information Age: Economy, Society and Culture.* Oxford: Blackwell.

CEDEFOP (2012) *Future skills supply and demand in Europe: Forecasts 2012.* Brussels: CEDEFOP.

Clarke, J. & Newman, J. (2012) 'The Alchemy of Austerity', *Critical Social Policy* 32 (2) 299-320.

Esping-Andersen, G. (1990) *The Three Worlds of Welfare Capitalism.* Cambridge: Polity.

Gamble, A. (2009) *Spectre at the Feast: capitalist crisis and the politics of recession.* Basingstoke: Palgrave.

Gove, M. (2011) Speech at Cambridge University 24th November 2011 available at
http://www.education.gov.uk/inthenews/speeches/a00200373/michael-gove-to-cambridge-university accessed March 2013

Gramsci, A. (1971) 'On Education' in *Selections from the Prison Notebooks*, ed Q. Hoare and G. Nowell-Smith. London: Lawrence & Wishart.

Hirtt, N. (2013, forthcoming) 'Education and training – under the dictatorship of the labour market' in K. Jones (ed.) *Education in Europe: the politics of austerity*. London: Radicaled.

James, C. (1973) *Young Lives at Stake*. New York: Schocken Books.

Jones, K. (2004) 'An old future, a new past: Labour remakes the English school' in R. Johnson and D. Steinberg (eds) *Blairism and the War of Persuasion: Labour's Passive Revolution*. London: Lawrence & Wishart.

Jones, K. (2013 forthcoming) 'The Right and the Left' in *Changing English: studies in reading and culture* (20) 4.

Jones, K. (2014a forthcoming) 'Conservatism and educational crisis: the case of England,' *Education Inquiry*.

Jones, K. (2014b forthcoming) 'The practice of radical education, from the welfare state to the neo-liberal order' in C. Burke and K. Jones (eds) *Education, Childhood and Anarchism: talking to Colin Ward*.

London Edinburgh Weekend Return Group (1980) *In and Against the State*. London: Pluto.

Mansell, W. (2012) 'Ofqual's apparent use of norm-referencing at

GCSE' website of National Association of Headteachers
http://www.naht.org.uk/welcome/news-and-media/key-topics/assessment/ofquals-apparent-use-of-norm-referencing-at-gcse/ 14th September.

Parr, C. (2013) '"Destination data" too narrow a path for schools', *Times Higher Education* http://www.timeshighereducation.co.uk/news/destination-data-too-narrow-a-path-for-schools/2002086.article 28th February.

Paton, G. (2013) 'Start Schooling later than age 5, say experts', *Daily Telegraph* 11th September.

Robin, C. (2011) *The Reactionary Mind: conservatism from Edmund Burke to Sarah Palin.* Oxford: Oxford University Press.

Rogoff, I. (2010) 'Education Actualised' *e-flux* 14/ 3/2010 http://www.e-flux.com/journal/%E2%80%9Ceducation-actualized%E2%80%9D-%E2%80%93-editorial/

Rustin, M. (2007) 'The Long Revolution Revisited', *Soundings* 35, March, 16-30.

School Without Walls (1978) *Lunatic Ideas: how newspapers treated education in 1977.* London: Corner House Bookshop.

Standing, G. (2011) *The Precariat: the new dangerous class.* London: Bloomsbury.

Thatcher, M. (1981) 'Mrs Thatcher: the first two years' (Interview with Ronald Butt), *Sunday Times,* 3rd May.

http://www.margaretthatcher.org/document/104475

Twigg, S. (2013) *No School Left Behind*
http://www.labour.org.uk/no-school-left-behind,2013-06-17
accessed 17th June.

Williams, R. (1961) *The Long Revolution*. Harmondsworth:
Penguin.

Contributors

Patrick Ainley is Professor of Education and Training at the University of Greenwich. He has published widely and also with Martin Allen.

Martin Allen is a writer, researcher and publisher. He has worked in secondary, sixth form and higher education and been active in the National Union of Teachers.

Valerie Coultas taught English for over 20 years in London schools. She is now Senior Lecturer in English in Education at Kingston University.

Richard Hatcher is Research Professor in Education at Birmingham City University and active in education politics locally in Birmingham and nationally.

Ken Jones is Professor of Education at Goldsmiths, University of London. He has edited 'Education in Europe: the politics of austerity', published by Radicaled in the autumn of 2013.

Clare Kelly was an early years and primary teacher in London schools for many years. She currently works at Goldsmiths, University of London.

Robin Simmons is Professor of Education at the University of Huddersfield.

John Yandell taught in inner London secondary schools for 20 years before moving to the London Institute of Education.

Values

Terra